HEARTFUL

PARENTING

Connec _____ *_____ung*

&

Emotional Intelligence

There is a secret ingredient to successful parenting. That ingredient is connectedness.

David E. Myers, Ph.D.

Heartful Parenting:

Connected Parenting & Emotional Intelligence

Published by:
Blue Bird Publishing
2266 S. Dobson #275
Mesa AZ 85202
(602) 831-6063
FAX (602) 831-1829
E-mail: bluebird @ bluebird1.com
Web site: http://www.bluebird1.com

Cover Design By:
Robin Graphic Designs

Cataloging-in-Publication Data

Myers, David E., 1945-
    Heartful parenting : connected parenting & emotional
    intelligence / David E. Myers.
        p.   cm.
    Includes bibliographical references.
    ISBN 0-933025-51-3
    1. Parenting--Psychological aspects. 2. Parents--
Psychology. 3. Parent and child. 4. Emotional maturity.
I. Title.
HQ755.8.M93 1996
649'.1--dc20   96-23796
                                                           CIP

CHILDREN

SPIRITED

ENERGETIC

FEELING

MYSTERIOUS

IMAGINATIVE

EXCITED

DREAMERS

LOVING

FILLED AND UNFULFILLED PROMISES

FEARFUL

GROWING

DIFFICULT

QUALITIES OF LIFE

Emotional Intelligence

EMPATHY

SELF-AWARENESS

EMOTIONAL MANAGEMENT

SELF-MOTIVATION

SOCIAL EFFECTIVENESS

Daniel Goleman defines emotional intelligence as:

> "Abilities such as being able to motivate oneself and persist in the face of frustrations; to control impulse and delay gratification; to regulate one's moods and keep distress from swamping the ability to think; to empathize and hope.[1]"

DEDICATED TO THOSE WHO SEEK TRUTH!

ACKNOWLEDGMENTS

There have been many people who have given me encouragement and assistance with this book over the years. I give thanks to Dr. James Pirkle, Rev. Joe Elmore, Karyn Zweifel, Mary Glasscock, Jane Roberts, Isie Hanson, Teresa Dixon, Jenny Smith, Dr. Carol Matlen, Dr. Dale Wisely, Dr. Sharon Gotlieb, David Jones, Dr. Michael Wesson, Donna Hamil, Dr. Nancy Wasson, Dr. Gerald Anderson, Dr. John Langlow, Kathy Miller, Kathleen Dutton, Dr. Edward Smith, Cari Sadlev,and Cheryl Deatrick. I offer apologies to any others whom I may have omitted.

Special thanks to Dr. Margaret Juliana and Donna Hunley who provided critical commentary, editorial suggestions, and ever increasing support. Donna's help was especially encouraging in the final phases of development.

I am very grateful to Cheryl Gorder who has given this work a chance and provided the guidance for final preparation of the manuscript.

Very special thanks to Jo Sherer who was profoundly encouraging and provided critical consultation throughout the writing. Jo has been the most important, consistent critic, cheerleader, and source of support across the writing of this book.

I also want to thank my very important teachers who have influenced my thinking and perceptions of life. I am deeply indebted to Dr. Jack Sadler, Dr. James Foulkes, Dr. Irma Shepherd, Dr. John Gamble, and Dr. Richard Felder.

I would also like to give thanks for the opportunity to learn from my stepchildren, Jason and Troy. They have taught me many invaluable lessons in relating and being connected.

TABLE OF CONTENTS

Introduction 9

Poet's Prayer 16

CHAPTER 1 17
Being Crazy, Loving and the Boiled Frog Syndrome

CHAPTER 2 26
What Makes People Tick

CHAPTER 3 41
General Guidelines for Parenting

CHAPTER 4 84
Establishing a Positive Relationship With Your Child

CHAPTER 5 113
Communication

CHAPTER 6 134
Emotionality

CHAPTER 7 163
Discipline

CHAPTER 8 176
The Growing Edge

CHAPTER 9 184
Professional Consultation

Lack of Connectedness: MLT's Personal Experience 196
Endnotes 199
Bibliography 202

Introduction

**Optimism and hope-like helplessness
and despair can be learned.[1]**

Heartful Parenting is a collection of my life's experiences that can be summarized by the beginning words of spirited, energetic, feeling, mysterious, excited, dreamers, loving, filled and unfulfilled promises, fearful, growing, and difficult. These are the qualities of life embodied by our children, and hopefully, ourselves. In the meantime, Daniel Goleman has written a book defining and suggesting that emotional intelligence may be more important than intellectual achievement. It is clear that connected parenting and emotional intelligence come together as we search for more connected aliveness—aliveness that includes empathy, self-awareness, emotional management, and social effectiveness (Goleman's attributes of emotional intelligence). The search for aliveness will embody all of life's qualities.

Of course, our lives would be more fulfilling with these attributes at our side. Our culture cries for this. Later in the book, you will see how MLT's life demonstrates this cry of disconnected experience. His disconnected childhood resulted in myriads of difficult emotions and behaviors. You will also see how he has struggled to end this generational legacy. As a culture, we must begin with the parenting of our children.

This book is for every one of you who has wished for a "school for parenting." In this "school" you will explore, think, and learn about positive parenting relationships, more effective communication, the positive use of emotions, and using discipline for effective teaching. As you accomplish this, connected living and emotional intelligence will be your source of inspiration.

Our children are our most valuable resource and treasure. I do not mean as objects, but as human beings who will also become parents. Their spirit will guide and shape the spirit of future generations. Most parents do acknowledge and realize the importance of their parenting; they also realize their parenting will be passed on to future generations. Consequently, these parents are committed to nurturing their children. In fact, many parents will do more for their children than for themselves. These parents often wonder about the "right" things to do and have many questions about the "how to's" of parenting. Doing the "right" thing and making daily decisions is very much a part of the parenting process.

When confronted with the depth and complexity of these questions, parents frequently focus on concrete goals for their children. While goals are useful, there are two major problems in using them as a primary focus. First, goals require a clear path for their achievement, and this is often absent. Secondly, concrete goals typically neglect the emotional, feeling aspects of human experience; the personal. With this focus, most parents overlook important emotional experiences within their child. This is then experienced as a neglect of their humanness, especially of their psychological needs. Without this realization, children become objects or possessions to be molded in someone else's image. Of course, this just creates resistance, resentment, and, worst of all, a feeling of psychological distance. This feeling of distance leads to detachment, feelings of separation, possibly depression, and a withdrawal from parents. Obviously, this withdrawal diminishes the sense of being connected to one's parents.

But when parents connect to the child's personal aspects (feelings, honest thinking, needs, perceptions), the focus changes. She will not feel as if she is an object or a possession to be molded in another's image.[2] She then will experience being loved for who she is and not because she has achieved some goal. Being loved for who she is will give her a sense of being whole and complete.

Without this sense, relating to herself and to others in a positive way is very difficult. She is not as likely to achieve goals in a positive way; she is likely to feel empty or as if something is missing. She is likely to have difficulties with empathy, self-awareness, relatedness, self-motivation, and emotional management—Goleman's Emotional Intelligence. The way you respond to her "insides" affects the feelings she has toward herself and the way she relates to others.

Your parental influence is powerful, especially as your child goes through very important developmental periods. You and she will have multitudes of experiences during these impressionable periods of life. Through these experiences you can contribute to her wholeness while helping her achieve goals. On the other hand, your child has the capacity to be very active, creative, and full of life. As a result, her behavior will, in turn, influence you. It is extremely important for you to realize that the internal reactions of parent and child are deeply intertwined. Through this realization, I would hope that you can find the sensitivity to allow your child's aliveness to develop as she journeys through the challenges of childhood. This sensitivity will increase your consciousness as well as your ability to connect.

This book is primarily written as a guide to enhance your sensitivity to the internal events of your child, so that you both might feel more whole and complete. This suggests a more personal, connected approach of looking at yourself and your child. As a result, your child will have a greater opportunity for developing her own connectedness and aliveness. She will have a chance to observe and develop emotional intelligence. She will not need drugs, distractions, promiscuous sex, or any other addictions to give her fulfillment. Both you and she have an opportunity to be enriched from a more personal experience of life.

This book is written to help you examine your parental feelings and behaviors. I believe there are at least five reasons for making this self-examination.

✓ You cannot do anything about what you do not know.

✓ Your parental feelings and behaviors set the atmosphere in the home.

✓ This examination will open you to the behaviors, thinking, feeling, and aliveness of your child.

✓ Your influence is likely to play a profound role in her adult life.

✓ You will live and encourage a fuller sense of life.

You have a penetrating influence on how she relates to herself. How she relates to herself will influence how she relates to her marriage partner. Goleman states, "Many or most emotional responses triggered so easily in marriage have been sculpted in childhood, first learned in our most intimate relationships or modeled for us by our parents."[3] How she relates to herself will also affect how she relates to her children and they with their children. This powerful influence has long-lasting effects. Looking at your influence requires becoming more conscious of internal events—yours and hers.

Internal consciousness affects life's decisions. It is clear she will make her own life decisions, and hopefully, she will take responsibility for her decisions. Your task is to provide her with an atmosphere in which she learns to make life's decisions with balanced sensitivity to herself and others. This sensitivity comes from how she balances her own internal events with the internal events of others. This balance requires a back and forth movement—from others to herself to others. With increasing awareness, you can become aware of your own back and forth movements.

Chapter 1 will provide you with a discussion of "Being Crazy, Loving, and the Boiled Frog Syndrome." It will enhance your sensitivity to the here and now of our culture as well as to the struggle of how we might better our lives. Chapter 2 reveals "What Makes People Tick," and you will find a discussion of behavior, thinking, emotions, and spirituality. Chapter 3 focuses on parenting guidelines and questions that will raise your awareness level as well as give you food for thought. You may want to take these questions slowly, possibly one area per day, until you have completed all twenty areas. Because no family is perfect, these questions are meant to raise your everyday consciousness, not make you more judgmental. Chapters 4, 5, 6, and 7 deal with guidelines in establishing a positive relationship, communication, emotionality, and discipline, respectively. From these guidelines, you can formulate your own responses to most emotional and behavioral situations. Chapter 8 is a summary of what I call the "Growing Edge" and highlights the most important aspects of the preceding chapters. Chapter 9 provides some general guidelines about when and whom you might consider for professional consultation. This could be one of the most important and difficult decisions you ever make.

This book is brief and to the point. It is written with guidelines intended for you to take time to self-examine, to consider how these ideas apply to your daily life. I have chosen to use the same conversational, down-to-earth language that I use in public speaking. As a result, you may experience a sense that I am talking directly to you and pointing to the basics of feeling more alive. Feeling more alive will allow you to live more authentically. This process begins with how each of us lives our aliveness, everyday. As we live our aliveness, our children can find strength in our vulnerability to feel and become their true selves.

This book is designed and written to empower you to be more connected—to find your own answers through a more connected viewing of your child. You may use your own experience as well as the experience of others. You will not always know what to do, as your child will be in a constant state of growth. I hope this gives you permission to be less knowing and to accept uncertain moments as opportunities to look deeply within yourself and your child. If you look deeply, I am sure you will find the wisdom of your own answers. In taking this deep, personal view, I hope that you will discover a deep "well" from which to draw love and understanding. As a result, you will feel more alive. As you enhance your experience and become more alive, you will sense that you are on a path, a path with heart. A path with heart is its own reward; it allows you to live life more fully. A path with empathy, self-awareness, balanced emotionality, self-motivation, and relatedness.

You may already have a professional guide as you struggle

with a particular difficulty or the meaning of your life. If so, my references to seeking therapy may or may not reflect your own experience. I believe you will find this book useful regardless of your decision to seek personal counseling.

HEARTFUL PARENTING

POET'S PRAYER

If I write another poem
let it be about love,
not the crazy love
we all start out writing about
but the love that keeps us sane,
the love that pain reveals
at a funeral
or when the doctor says what we don't want to hear;
the love that men won't talk about,
the love of divorced people
when they find their way back to marriage;
the love of an old family place
when the generations gather there;
the love of old friends
who realize they're the only ones left;
and the love of children,
not only when they are smiling or sleeping
or clean or straight or strong or smart,
but when they are none of those things
and need more love than anyone can give,
and cannot even recognize the love they get.[1]

Chapter 1

BEING CRAZY, LOVING
& THE BOILED FROG SYNDROME

"Life is difficult."[1]

"If young people do not have a feeling of connectedness with other human beings and if they have
no empathy, guilt, shame or sense of responsiblility,
then ultimately the value of human life will be lost.[2]

There are many different kinds of people in the world. Some
are kind, generous, and loving. Others are mean and violent. Some
march to the beat of a different drummer, and some march in a very
conventional manner. Certainly, this raises age-old questions— "Why
do people do what they do? Why do they make certain choices?" I
do not know a whole lot about the "why's" of these choices, but I do
know about personal experience. I know about my own personal
experience, and I know about the personal experience of many others. As a therapist, I have had the honor of sharing in many individuals' lives. These individuals have told of how their lives were influenced, how they thought and felt, and what decisions they made as a
result of these influences. They also shared how their sense of connectedness[3] was affected. While there are many influences (eg.
school, peers, church) parenting is the primary influence in connectedness. Parenting is the foundation for the shaping of lives.

17

So, as life is difficult, losses of connectedness make life even more difficult. There is a shortage of connectedness among human beings and with their environment. We are in very crazy times.

CRAZY TIMES

Pause and think about the craziness of these times. You may bring to mind instances of events which make little or no sense to you. A recent example for me was the case of an injured teacher protecting one of his children. His school board initially ruled that protecting the child was irrelevent to his duties. Thank goodness, public outcry caused the board to reverse their decision! In the same vein, an Oregon Supreme Court was required to rule (1996) that a man who left his armored truck to save a woman from a knife-bearing attacker could not be terminated. These clearly are instances of craziness in our times.

Thus, crazy events do not refer to the experience of psychiatric patients. However, many psychiatric patients carry the effects of this craziness. When they are hospitalized, their hospitalization is frequently an effort to recover and cope with the after-effects of craziness.

In this book, I am not talking about a psychiatric diagnosis. I am talking about the craziness of our culture that is universally tolerated and even accepted as a substitute for real connectedness. I am talking about the craziness of not making sense, being mean, denying reality, and portraying the world as a storybook fantasy.

This craziness (in both mild and severe forms) is quite pervasive in our culture. My concern is how hurtful this craziness has become to all of us, even when it is not intentional. Although I do not have a definitive answer for this difficulty, I can offer guidance for finding your own connectedness. As you and others are more connected, this craziness can be handled in more constructive ways. Our intense, constructive efforts to heal through connectedness could make a real difference in this culture.

CRAZINESS VS. CONFUSION

One reviewer of this writing suggested that I use the word "confusion" instead of "craziness." I thought and thought, but "confusion" just did not feel right. It doesn't convey how much craziness hurts people. With confusion, people are more apt to stop and think about their actions. Being confused also implies motivation for positive behavior change without the knowledge of what to do or how to change. I do not sense any such positive motivation in craziness. With craziness, people just continue not making sense, being mean, denying reality, and portraying the world as a storybook fantasy.

Also, there is less awareness in craziness. Thus, its impact is more subtle, extensive, and harder to foresee. Because it is less likely to be noticed, the craziness and its damage become more pervasive. This is not to say that visible damage is harmless. But people are more likely to do something about damage they can see than damage they can not see. People are profoundly influenced and scarred by the craziness they can and can not see. We need to be more aware so that we can change craziness to a more connected, loving, concerned way of being. **We need to be more aware.**

HOW CRAZINESS HURTS, FIVE CRAZY WAYS

There are many examples of this hurtful and serious craziness. It is fairly common knowledge that abused children often become abusive parents. This feels crazy in that children are not in this world to be abused. Furthermore, one would expect these adults to remember how it felt to be abused and not to repeat this tragedy. Unfortunately, this is not their reality. Where is their awareness of this craziness?

School violence is another crazy behavior. *USA Today* [4] cited a survey reporting one in four schools with deaths or serious injuries. School violence was reported to have increased 38% in the surveyed communities; 70% of surveyed communities assign local police to their schools; 90% send police to school athletic events. What is happening with and to these children? A recent major news magazine headlined "Teenage Time Bombs—Violent juvenile crime is soaring and it's going to get worse."[5] What is creating these violent tendencies? How will these children be as adults? Not only is school violence crazy, it is terrifying.

Sexual abuse is another crazy behavior. It is common knowledge that women who are raped suffer intense emotional aftereffects. It seems crazy to me that men would want to inflict such injuries on women. *Newsweek* [6] reported that the United States has a rape rate twenty times higher than in Japan. On a worse note, *Time*[7] reported that "a fourth of the boys and a sixth of the girls said it was acceptable for a man to force a woman to kiss him or have sex if he spent money on her." *Harpers*[8] reported that 86% of 13 to 15-year-old boys said "that it was acceptable for a man to rape his wife." What kind of relationships do these individuals really want? What kind of relationships will they have? What kind of culture produces these results? What is behind the use of force for what should be an intensely, beautiful act of love? Obviously, these are not acts of love. Where is the awareness of this craziness?

The amount of lying that occurs in our culture is also crazy. There are books[9,10,11] that reveal that we all tell lies, that there is serious lying, and that explore the nature of lying. Depending on your view, this is either normal, mildly hurtful or seriously hurtful. I am of the belief that we decry lying and yet may be prone to do this in certain situations. Of course, this does not make it right. Saxe suggests that there is serious lying in relationships (this probably does not surprise you) as well as in academics. Saxe states, " Each of us has ways of justifying lies, and in part, the behavior results from seeing the world in a way that makes the behavior acceptable."[12] He further suggests that we need to be clearer about the "conditions for honesty" as well as understanding the nature of differences in perception (among people). *Time* [13] headlined on their front cover, "Lying—Everybody's Doing It (Honest)." *USA Today*[14] headlined that "Cheating, Lying on the Rise" and reports troubling findings related to honesty. Demanding that people tell the truth does not seem to help raise the amount of truthfulness. Lying is a major component of craziness.

I would like to provide you with a fifth example of serious and hurtful craziness. That is drug usage, and the way we deal with it in this culture. We continue a "war on drugs" with the "Just Say NO" campaign, and yet the war is reported to be lost. *U.S. News and World Report*[15] provides figures that drug use among teenagers has risen since 1992. It seems crazy that we are not offering individuals adequate alternatives to drugs. Also, there is little publicity about the fundamental **causes** of our drug epidemic. Is an easy answer of "NO" going to take care of the problem? How is it that drug users forget how crazy drugs are? If we are perfectly honest with ourselves, we know the answer to this question.

IS IT THAT SIMPLE?

"Just Say NO" implies an easy answer. Telling people to be honest ought to convince them that this is the right thing to do. Teaching people about child and sexual abuse "should" stop this problem. These ideas imply simple solutions. I wish it could be this simple. In fact, none of this is simple. Connectedness among people is quite complex. Feeling empathy and concern for others is quite complex. The truth is, our culture continues to deny and avoid the complexity of this.

Consequently, the culture then looks for simple solutions to very complex problems. This doesn't make sense, this is mean, this denies reality, and this portrays the world as a storybook fantasy. As a result, individuals within our culture deny and avoid the complexity of their own lives. They may sense that something is wrong, but lack adequate resources for further exploration. Each individual who denies and avoids is a symptom of a culture that denies and avoids. As a result, craziness tends to create more craziness.

This is hurtful. Hurtfulness "should" nurture connectedness with deep levels of caring, loving, and understanding. Maybe, one on one, there could be a greater awareness and experience of real connectedness. **Connectedness is the fertile ground for healing**.

SUBTLE CRAZIES: AN EPIDEMIC

Dishonesty, school violence, child, sex, and drug abuse are clearly serious problems in which denial and avoidance play a major role. There are also many problems that don't appear to be quite so serious, but in reality are. I am now talking about the problems that develop from parent-child interactions that do not make sense, are mean, deny reality, or portray the world as some sort of storybook fantasy.

Please consider the following examples: A man who will not commit to a relationship because he fears an unknown outcome; a woman who continues to choose men who do not commit; a woman who now has trouble with eating because this was the major pleasurable event in her childhood; a child who refuses to perform in school as a way of retaliation; a man who has affairs because he feels inadequate in a meaningful relationship; a woman who is very neat, tidy and cannot stand to have anything out of place; a man who does not finish college because he is struggling with feelings of inferiority—the result of his never being allowed to speak his inner truth as a child; and finally, a very successful businessman who is afraid that he will be "found out" to be an imposter. You probably know someone who is or has experienced one or more of these dificulties.

As you consider these examples of individual problems, you can easily see that each problem affects self and others. These individuals have difficulty connecting with themselves and with others. Their seemingly "minor" problems are, in fact, very serious. They are deeply hurtful. Sadly, they are also very common, so common that numerous books are written about these difficulties. So common, that for me, the high frequency symbolizes the seriousness of the cultural craziness. Craziness and hurtfulness are contagious. We are all affected.

As I suggested earlier, this craziness can result in psychiatric disturbances. While there may be other predisposing factors, environmental factors play a role in our mental health. Another survey reported in *USA Today* [16] reported "Nearly half of people ages 15-54 have experienced at least one bout with a psychiatric disorder, and about 1 in 3 have had such an episode over the last year." Another result: "Men are nearly twice as likely as women to have a substance abuse/dependence problem during their lives—35% vs.18% of women. Women are more vulnerable to depression—21% vs. 13% for men." A later study found that "worker's depression costs $43 billion a year" to industry.[17] These findings are striking, and suggest a need for careful analysis of individual experience. Psychological pain is abundant. I would ask you to consider the implication of these findings as our culture makes decisions—decisions affecting the personal experience of each of us.

There is another important form of "crazy" that I would like to mention. Perhaps, it is the major underlying craziness in our culture; perhaps, it is based on the human need for control. Almost every one of us carries the belief that we earn love through achievement. We may not openly acknowlege this belief, but we act upon it everyday. This is the opposite of our deserving love simply because we exist. Pause and think for a moment about the differences between earning love and deserving love. There are many, many people who feel that they are not deserving of love unless they **do** something that merits approval. This is often true for people who are high achievers.

Earning love falls within my definition of craziness. I believe it does not make sense, it is mean, and it creates a culture of people who feel they can only be loved if they do enough of the "right" thing. If this is real love, then our culture does not have a chance. I know there is a large group of people who believe that we must encourage and reward achievement. I do not disagree. However, there can be and **is** a feeling of love that transcends encouragement and reward. A true feeling of love can connect people in a very powerful way. Without it, there is not enough real love to bind us together as a culture.

BEING MORE CONNECTED

Connectedness is the opposite of hurtful craziness. I am talking about a feeling toward others and one's self that allows us to be more caring, more loving. I am talking about our need to relate in warm, sharing ways to help us feel more personally competent. Access to our inner experience begins the process of healing. With this access, we can feel connected and loving. We can know the hurt of others and use this pain to guide us. We can experience more fully the joys and struggles of our children. We can remember and use our memories to connect wisely with our children. We can understand our difficulties and use these difficulties as motivation for change. We can fully realize that we have a conscious as well as an unconscious side. We can accept that we may not always know what love means, but we can evolve. Only then can we use this experience to help our children to love and be connected with others.

As a result, we cannot just be interested in others, we must develop connectedness with ourselves. From this connected interest in ourselves and others, we can then work toward a truly balanced sense of loving. We can grow. We can lovingly influence some of what happens to our children. We can acquire a true understanding of the personal experiences within each of us. We must not stop at the superficial level if we are to truly know ourselves and others. If we are mindful and if we feel these personal experiences, we can then know the **connectedness** that will lessen our culture's "crazies." We will then live life more fully.

ABOUT THE BOILED FROG, THE HEAT IS ON!

You are probably wondering, "What has all of this to do with the boiled frog syndrome?" Well, the boiled frog syndrome, as I understand it, is the experience of placing a frog in water and gradually turning up the heat. If the story is correct, this frog will not realize that the water is getting hotter and hotter. Eventually, the frog will die from the heat despite being able to leave the water at anytime. The obvious moral is that the "temperature" is getting hotter in our culture. Our inability to fully detect the change in temperature is the result of our superficial understanding and our unwillingness to look at the long-range effects of personal experience.

I invite you to open your heart as you think about these words.

You see, just as hurtfulness begets hurtfulness, loving begets loving. Then, we can lower the temperature.

Chapter 2

WHAT MAKES PEOPLE TICK

Life is a mystery. With this in mind, it seems "nervy" that I am going to try to tell you what makes people tick, especially when I know how complicated people are. However, I have learned some things over the years which may help. I would like to emphasize that my thoughts are not new; they are an integration of learning from many different resources. My aim is to help clarify how you and your children operate in this world. As you read this, you will find a great deal of overlap. In my version of what makes people tick, everything in human behavior is directly or indirectly connected to everything else.

BASIC PARTS

For the sake of simplicity, I would like to categorize human behavior into four basic parts. The first part is probably the easiest to talk about, the part everybody sees: **external behavior**. This consists of what is seen on the outside of your child's skin. You can see her walk, you can hear her talk, and you can know if she went to bed. You can know if a certain external behavior did or did not happen. However, you may not know why the behavior happened (this question has plagued philosophers for years). Some believe that external behavior is controlled by what happens outside a person's skin (external). Clearly, there are outside influences. In my version, your child's behavior (and yours) is ultimately influenced by what happens **inside** her skin (internal).

What you believe strongly affects your parenting attitude and your willingness to understand your child's personal process (her insides). If you believe behavior is most affected by outside sources, you will focus on external consequences such as rewards and punishments. If you believe behavior comes from within, you will mostly focus on her thoughts, feelings, and spirit. As you recognize and understand the internal processing of humans, you are more likely to be empathetic, collaborative, and successful in achieving desired goals. Personal understanding acknowledges your sense of her as a human being and not as an object to be molded in your image.

This brings me to the three remaining parts of a person, all internal. The first is **thinking**. Nobody can actually see or hear this except for the person who is doing the thinking. Words like "believe," "opinion," "consider," "ponder," "remember," "judge," and "reason" refer to things that occur in this category. Thinking is used to rehearse future events, evaluate past events, solve problems, and to just imagine. Thinking can be a very creative process, or it can be the "playing back" of messages that an individual previously received. Using thinking to understand these messages is a very important aspect of appreciating the influence of past events.

Thinking is an aspect of human behavior that is highly valued. Thinking allows me to come up with words which are translated into messages that go to my fingers, which then push the buttons on the computer's keyboard. Pushing the buttons is the external behavior which comes from my thinking.

The next inside part is **feeling** or **emotion**. Some people make a distinction between feelings and emotions: I do not. Related words are "sensation" and "passion." More specifically, feelings (or emotions) refer to a stirring on the inside which gives rise to such sensations as anger, sadness, happiness, hatred, joy, love, anxiety, eagerness, and so on. These sensations are experienced in the physical body, whereas thinking is more of the mind. I have found these words do not reflect the internal experience very well, since feelings are much more alive than the words used to describe them. However, they do serve as symbols of the sensation each of us feels when there is a physical stirring. *Roget's Thesaurus* (Third Edition) provides some additional help with words that point to emotional experiences. It is worth noting that our feelings are most often attached to "heart" words: "inmost heart," "heart's core," "bottom of the heart," "deep sense," "tender feelings," and "tender heart." This is because we think of our hearts as central to life and of feelings as central to the experience of life. In fact, emotions are the lifeblood of living life fully. Thus, to experience life fully, you must feel your internal life through experiencing your emotional energies. Without your feelings, life consists of thinking and external behavior; it is **flat**. Many people have described their experience as numb, sort of like Novocaine. The lack of feelings is often referred to as "hardhearted."

The last and most important part, and the one most difficult to talk about, is our **spirit**. The experience of spirit is referred to as spirituality. Marion Woodman, a Jungian analyst, has defined spirituality as being "full of the spirit." James and James[1] believe, "The wonders of the human spirit motivate us to reach out toward specific goals." "Urges of the human spirit are to live, to be free, to understand, to create, to enjoy, to connect, and to transcend." For me, I feel spiritual when my inner world totally connects with my outer world—I call this oneness. Wonderful creativity is often accompanied by an experience of spirituality. Oneness and creativity give a true experience of aliveness. When spirituality truly happens, it is such a powerful experience, and there are very few words, if any, to adequately describe the experience. However, we can know by the transcending power of the experience whether it is indeed spiritual.

As an example, I'd like to tell you about an incident that occurred to me many years ago. After doing some therapy work, I was standing in New Hampshire looking into a beautiful lake surrounded by magnificent trees. As I stood there, I could feel what I call "God energy" entering my feet and traveling up through my body into my head. I felt powerfully connected to the universe. This spirituality felt like energy from a higher being. You may name this higher being according to your own religious beliefs. What matters is sensing this extraordinary level of energy and knowing its connection to a higher level of existence, or higher being.

You might call it a transcendence. You might call it soul,

zest, animation, heart, force from above, vitality, or a will to live. It is a feeling of fullness and oneness that goes way beyond the three basic parts of behaving, thinking, and feeling. To consistently have this higher sense of spirit, your three basic parts must work well together. This means a strong energy flow between your basic parts and consciousness of any conflict. Conflict or blockage of energy between parts tends to reduce spirituality. Your spirituality is strongly affected by the freedom of your energy flow.

> **It has been urged that man's spiritual life is the emergence in him of a new level of experience, a new integration of the aesthetic, intellectual and moral elements in his nature . . . In it the whole personality is involved, in both its inward completeness and its outward relationships.[2]**

There are many ideas of how to **enhance** your parts working together, and there are many ideas of how to **enhance** your spirituality. I invite you to explore your own sense of spirituality. This exploration is vital in having a sense of balance between yourself, others, and the environment.

In summary, the four basic parts to your being are external behavior, thinking, feeling, and spirituality. How these four parts work together gives you your experience of life. These four parts are connected and probably are so connected that calling them by different names is somewhat absurd. Personally, I do not believe in the separation of mind and body. I could just as easily call them energies. The amount of energy in each of these parts depends on how much you acknowledge and nurture each part. This nurturing, in turn, depends on what you learned from previous experiences. The amount of energy you experience will give you the fuel for your sense of spirituality. This will connect you with your higher being and with what most people refer to as God. As you feel these energies, they, in turn, will have a tremendous impact on your child—she will feel

her energies. Her energies will then give her a sense of connectedness and a feeling of being in touch with her "higher being."

HISTORY: HEREDITY AND LEARNING

As a human being, you began your development at concep-
tion. At that point, heredity and the environment in your mother's
womb were the two most important factors in your development.
These are important, long-lasting factors. From the point of concep-
tion, you and every other human being have a history. When a child
is born, she leaves the mother's womb and enters the external world.
At this point, the two most influential factors become heredity and
the environment of the **external** world. There is a strong interaction
between heredity and learning. A child is born with numerous innate
potentials which are a function of heredity. Many of these potentials
are modified through learning.

As a result, much of human behavior is an interaction between heredity and learning. Medical views tend to place a higher
value on physical, inherited characteristics; psychological views tend
to place a higher value on what is learned through experience. There
is no doubt that there are many inherited characteristics, some of
which are relatively unchangeable. However, as a child goes through
life, experience affects her emotionally, her sense of relationship,
and her views of life. What is this experience that has such a profound effect?

Generally, our culture views experience as external, involving those things that happen **to** us. School is an experience. Going
to a movie is an experience. Being praised is an experience. But
what goes on inside as these individuals experience these external
events? From the previous section, you will remember that individuals think, feel, and are spiritual. To simplify, I would like to
refer to all that goes on inside an individual as **internal processing**.
Internal processing includes the various experiences that make up
thinking, feeling, and spirituality.

Internal processing is fundamental to how each of us decides
to relate to ourselves and others. Here is an example that illustrates

internal processing: You are bothered by your child's refusal to eat. This means you have thoughts and feelings about her not eating. These are your inside experiences. There could be many different combinations of thoughts and feelings. You might, for example, think your child is not getting the proper nutrition, or you might think she is being stubborn. Or you might have memories of what it was like for you as a child to have dinner with your family. You might be thinking your child will not eat because you are her parent. Any of these thoughts are possible.

You may also be having any combination of feelings. You might be sad and tearful that an opportunity of positive interaction has not taken place. You might feel frustrated or even angry that your child is not cooperating. You might feel helpless and rejected that she does not want to eat. If you are having childhood eating memories, you may have a resurgence of feeling associated with these memories.

As you can see, there can be any number of thoughts and feelings that can go into this experience. Your unique combination of thoughts and feelings in the moment of your child's refusal to eat is your internal processing. It is **your** experience. This experience then becomes part of your history. Fortunately or unfortunately, this experience also becomes part of your child's experience which affects the development of her four basic parts. Her history contains the development of her four basic parts.

Up to now, I have talked only about your internal processing and how this becomes a part of your child's history. Of course, if the process is internal, you may well be wondering how it affects your child. Your internal processing affects her at two levels, the unconscious and the conscious. At the unconscious level, your child's sensitive unconscious can pick up cues of what is going on in your internal processing. Her unconscious reads your unconscious. This is scary since these happenings are out of your awareness. Regardless of your intentions, much does occur outside of your awareness.

At the conscious level, your internal processing is going to influence your external behavior. For instance, your processing might lead to your saying or doing nothing about her refusal to eat. Your processing might lead you to be very gentle in your mannerisms and words. Another combination of thoughts and feelings might lead you to show anger. Whatever you show will then lead to a combination of thoughts and feelings in your child.

Her combination of thoughts and feelings will then lead her to a certain external behavior. She might show frustration, sadness, a stubborn refusal, or a willingness to eat depending on her internal processing. Thus, you affect your child, and your child affects you. It may seem as if you are controlling one another, but that is not the case. You each control your own responses. Both you and your child may choose to respond in any number of ways. Your choice of responses may affect her choice, and vice-versa. With internal processing, either of you can **choose** to break the chain of events.

Internal processing is the vital link between what occurs on the inside of human beings (thinking and feelings) and what occurs on the outside (behavior). What you do on the inside of yourself influences what you do on the outside. This, in turn influences others. Internal events affect external happenings, and external happenings affect internal events. Even though the experience is powerful, internal processing gives individuals the opportunity to make choices.

This is not startling news, and yet people often forget this very simple truth. When individuals acknowledge this truth, their relationships can be healthier and more connected.

There are millions of experiences in a lifetime, and every time something happens to us, that something is recorded in our bodies as historical data. We have recorded things that have been done to us, things we saw done, things we did to others, and things we did to ourselves. We may not remember each of our experiences, but these experiences accumulate and give us a sense of ourselves (contributing to self-esteem and wholeness) in different situations. We may or may not be conscious of how the experiences have affected us.

At a personal level, your recorded experience is your history. Your history may be relatively pleasant, possibly joyous, or it may be mildly to seriously traumatic. It is likely you have had good times as well as bad. You may have an easier time handling the good than the bad. However, there are people who have a difficult time with the good. If you examined their recorded experiences carefully, you might be able to discover why this is the case. Often, these individuals are more prepared through experience to deal with "bad" times.

A series of mildly difficult circumstances or even one extremely traumatic event can push children into using coping mechanisms that involve excessive fear, resentment, and denial. As a parent, you can do your best to limit the difficult situations, but it is impossible to prevent all of them. It is also not within your power to prevent all tragic happenings. It is within your power to do your best to minimize the possibility of traumatic events. It is also within your power to help your child experience psychological healing.

Part of parenting is teaching her how to process life experiences, experiences that make up her history. With your help and example, she can learn to process most of life's events so that these experiences "pass on through" without leaving any "permanent" disabling impact. By this, I mean there will be recorded memories but little, if any, effect at the personality level. How your child processes life's events will play a large role in her personality development.

PASSING ON THROUGH AND POWER

I have been talking to you about your child's experiences and how experiences are the essence of personal history. And yes, a portion of that history will involve suffering of some sort. Your task is to teach her skills to handle this suffering so she is not "permanently" affected. In other words, so that her sensitivity toward herself or others is not damaged. I see this as emotional healing. Sometimes the healing occurs without much effort, and sometimes healing requires extraordinary and on-going efforts. Basically, emotional healing is natural, much like the physical healing of a cut. However, we have learned that there are things that aid the healing of a cut. My sense is that the same is true for emotional healing. Because there is so much cultural denial and avoidance, outside help and encouragement are often required for natural healing. This is true for adults as well as for children.

As humans experience life, they record these experiences either at the conscious or the unconscious level. If a particular event or a series of events are mildly difficult, a person is likely to heal by experiencing his thoughts and feelings fully. These thoughts and feelings may or may not result in a change of external behavior. If the four basic parts (external behavior, thinking, feeling, and spirituality) are experienced fully and consciously, the event is likely to pass on through.

For example, in the case of a death, **active** grieving is healing. If grief is denied or unexpressed, depression is likely. Because the event is not fully experienced by the four parts, the event is recorded at the unconscious level and does not pass on through. This is called "blocking." Using the same example, **inhibiting** grief blocks the flow of emotional energy and can lead to depression. When the event is not acknowledged fully, is minimized, or is not allowed to have a physical expression, the experience does not go to completion and remains unfinished. Tremendous energy is required to keep unfinished business out of awareness. With unfinished business, people describe sensations such as yearnings, naggings, or emotional ghosts.

My sense is that most situations that are somewhat difficult can be handled by allowing all of the energies to "pass on through," as long as the individual is open to the event being fully experienced. When fully experienced, a sense of calm and wholeness follows the completion of the experience. Then an individual is free to go on to the next experience. The accumulation of these healing experiences strengthens the use of natural healing, and lessens the conflict between the four basic parts. Of course, this lessens anxiety and increases self-esteem.

A particular event or a series of mildly difficult events may also be called mildly powerful. Power is the intensity of the event. With mild degrees of power, there is less likely to be long-lasting effects than with larger degrees of power (intensity). For example, you are more likely to be affected by a child's tears than by hearing about her sadness without the tears. Tears provide more power and intensity to the experience of sadness. Another example, your children are likely to respond very differently to a spanking than to having their movie privileges taken away. This does not mean that spanking is more effective. You have no way of knowing for certain what is mild and what is intense within your child. As a result, it is important that you model constructive "passing on through" experiences. Your emotional expressions will encourage her to be more emotionally and verbally expressive.

Let me now give you an example which cuts both ways. That is, I thought I was being a leader in constructive expression, but my children taught me a most valuable lesson. Many years ago, our family lost a much-loved dog. The children cried intensely and expressed loud anger over the loss. I served as an encouraging parent and affirmed their feelings as they expressed them. It was loud and intense. After a while, they went out to play, while I quickly noticed a nagging, depressed feeling. After experiencing this feeling for two weeks, I realized I had not allowed myself to grieve. After I allowed myself to experience my grief, the nagging, depressed feeling then disappeared. My children "taught" me the power of natural healing and what happens when it is not allowed.

PERSONALITY

As she develops, your child is learning different behaviors, more advanced and complex ways of thinking, and to allow certain feelings to be expressed. Hopefully, she is learning that there are constructive and destructive ways to express these feelings. As she learns more about thinking, feelings, and behavior her spirituality either develops or is modified. She learns that her four basic parts work together, or she learns when they do not. These are the experiences of your child. She may have some awareness of these parts, or she may be operating at a level where she is just performing. Or she may have a good sense of being in the world with confidence. Whichever of these is the case, she is developing qualities that influence the way she goes through life. These qualities can be sensed by others and herself.

These qualities are the ingredients of her personality. The thesaurus for this computer program gives the words "character," "demeanor," "disposition," "nature," and "temperament" as synonyms. Although these words add meaning to the idea and much is written about personality, I would like to give you my simplified version. More specifically, I would like to discuss the prominent aspects that come from within a person, develop through experience, and have an effect on others.

For me, two words provide a basis for the experience of personality. These words refer to an inner experience of personality and can only be sensed indirectly. The two words are "self-esteem" and "wholeness." I use **self-esteem** to define how you value yourself. This sense is global. It can range from either liking or not liking yourself to thinking you can never do anything right. It includes such things as whether or not you are "loveable" to whether or not you have confidence in yourself. Thus, self-esteem relates to how you evaluate yourself in general. You may sense your self-esteem as high, or you may deem it low. Whatever your evaluation, my experience suggests self-esteem is related to how your four basic parts work together. How your parts work together is dependent upon how you process your experience.

The second word is **wholeness** and refers to how you operate psychologically. Wholeness refers to being complete, unfragmented, undamaged, and holy. Again, if your four basic parts work well together, you are likely to have a sense of wholeness. At this point, I would like to make a simple clarification of the four basic parts. That is, each basic part is made up of subparts. For example, your behavior part is made up of such subparts as eating, sleeping, playing, and so on; your thinking part is made up of such subparts as analyzing, remembering, and so on; and your feeling part is made up of such subparts as anger, sadness, and so on. As you think about these subparts, your awareness of them increases.

The problem is, we do not think or feel enough to be fully conscious of these "workings." Generally speaking, we do not want to fully acknowledge or feel the intensity of our insides. If you feel any subpart of you is too intense, bad or needs to be discarded, then

it is pushed to the back of your mind where it can become unconscious. The subpart "waits" to give you either firm or vague signals
of its presence. This creates conflict and often anxiety. Since the
subpart must remain hidden, you can not be your real self. Psychological depression can easily arise. Keeping subparts of yourself
hidden then prevents you from feeling whole.

At the same time, knowing there are destructive parts does
not give you permission to let them out in any way you desire. You
can deal with your destructive parts in a way which provides wholeness. Destructive subparts are an aspect of every human's existence.
By understanding and emotionally dealing with these destructive
parts, you can acquire wholeness. To experience full self-esteem
and wholeness, you must own or reclaim all of your subparts. This
may be quite painful, and it may require outside help. The process of
interaction among your subparts is essential to a sense of high self-
esteem and wholeness. Self-esteem and wholeness are major con-
tributors to personality.

As subparts or aspects of personality grow from the accumulation of experience, personality aspects develop and accumulate
across time. Different levels (or experience) of each aspect will
result in differing personality traits. One aspect I have mentioned is
sensitivity. Sensitivity refers to the extent someone is aware of her
internal and external happenings. In my way of thinking, sensitivity
is good so long as you do not overreact and are willing to check out
(discuss) your feelings with others.

Another aspect of personality is anger. Many people use anger to control their own feelings and the behaviors of others. Anger
is good when it is a way of constructively taking care of yourself; for
example, when it is a response to a real threat. The danger occurs
when some people feel threatened but really are not. They then may
be fearful, frustrated, angry, and possibly aggressive. Frustration
and aggression are often part of an angry personality type.

Sensitivity and anger play a role in how someone is forceful.
People who are forceful can be sensitive; but forceful people who
lack sensitivity are often seen as aggressive. Aggressive behavior
follows not caring about what others think and feel, especially if

boundaries are violated.

The complexity of sensitivity, forcefulness, and anger requires further illustration. Someone who is sensitive and forceful will attend to her thoughts and feelings, attempt to attend to the other's thoughts and feelings, and will respectfully assert her inside processing. A person who is sensitive and not forceful will attend to the inside processing of herself and others, but will not assert her thoughts and feelings. A person who is forceful but not sensitive will assert herself in disrespect of the other person. Disrespect usually includes name calling, put-downs, physical violations, unwillingness to listen, intense manipulations, and so on.

You can be sensitive, forceful, and express your anger respectfully. You can be sensitive, not forceful, and "rage" when you no longer can contain your anger. You can be insensitive, not forceful, and excessively contain your anger. By now, you can easily see that sensitivity, forcefulness, and anger may be expressed in any number of ways. How they manifest is determined by the way you perceive yourself and what you do with your perception. How they are expressed determines how others will experience you. These are significant aspects of personality. Please ask yourself, how am I sensitive and how am I forceful? Second, when and how do I express anger?

Anger and sensitivity play a role in whether or not someone is physically or psychologically violent. If someone loses sensitivity in anger, then anger can easily result in name calling, put downs, or physical actions like pushing, hitting, and restraining against the other's wishes. This behavior is violent and a violation of the other's boundaries. Obviously, it does not promote mutual relating.

Someone may be angry, yet sensitive enough to limit name calling, put-downs, and physical expressions. However, the attempts at limiting anger may result in difficulties in speaking one's mind. Often, these energies build until this type of individual barks at others, rather than releasing anger constructively. These individuals may also have a tendency to want to punish and get even for perceived wrongs in the world. Some people become skeptical and cynical, when they limit their anger.

At the other extreme, there are those who would not "hurt a fly." These individuals are either independent (can take care of themselves) or are dependent (want others to take care of them). Some individuals can be both independent and dependent depending on the situation. Individuals often struggle with balancing dependency and independence. Dependency can be unwelcome, OK, or it can even be good, depending on the circumstances. For example, many dependent children leave home prematurely (thinking they are independent), and later return to their parental home. Some dependent people play the role of being helpless, even of being a victim. On the surface, it would seem that these people do not have much power, yet their ability to get others to rescue them gives them a great deal of power. By draining other people's energies, excessively dependent people can "hurt a fly." Others who wouldn't "hurt a fly" give in to the demands and guilt-tripping of others. These individuals are easy marks for the forceful; they would rather not fight, and, some do not even want to struggle. They are often referred to as spineless, and rarely evoke respect from others.

There is also a group of people who would "hurt a fly," but this would bother them (sensitive and forceful). These individuals can take action, but they understand their reasons and do not go out of their way to harm anyone. They are sensitive but realize hurt as a possible part of any interaction. They do their best to be balanced and yet do not cower when confronted by other people. They are respectful, friendly, and able to use their feelings constructively. They are open to outside input when they need to be open, and closed when they need to be closed. They are able to make decisions and hold their impulsiveness to a minimum.

These are my simplified ideas of certain personality aspects learned through experience. Personality aspects encourage being open or closed. As each child develops, she learns in her own way and time what is safe, what is acceptable, and what she can and cannot rebel against. All of this comes from the interaction of her internal processing: her feelings and thoughts as they affect and are affected by the external world.

What makes people tick? Several factors are involved: how

they relate inside themselves to their thoughts, feelings, and behavior; how they sense their spirituality; how they relate to others; how they make conscious and unconscious choices. We each need to monitor the manner in which we relate so that we can be more connected to one another. In being more connected, we can have more fulfilling, balanced lives. Then, we can make significant changes in our culture. The task is great. We can each start with the people closest to us. If we really become more conscious of our inner reality, and if we become more loving, there is a chance to deal with the craziness of this culture. Or at the very least, we can begin to exchange alienation for a greater sense of connection.

Chapter 3

GENERAL GUIDELINES FOR PARENTING

"Why is it we know so little about ourselves yet expect so much from others? We refuse to recognize the flimsy curtain that separates the intention from the result, the image from reality."[1]

The following chapter consists of a series of parenting guidelines helpful in your daily thinking and consciousness. They will clarify your parenting interactions. I would suggest reading one per day with your spouse (or significant other person) and discussing your responses. You can then mull over your mutual responses and make specific parenting decisions. The aim of these discussions is to enhance intimacy between the two of you. If you observe major differences in opinions that cannot be resolved, please consider seeking professional consultation. **Your child's psychological life is too important to risk.** If you do not have a significant other person, you might want to put your thoughts on paper.

At the end of each section, you will find information on "Pitfalls." This is a note to alert you to possible complications while practicing the Guideline. As you might guess, practicing life with more consciousness can be quite difficult. The guidelines will help you to be more aware, provide a structure for thinking about problems, and allow you to be more alive and connected. As you become more alive, you will be more connected to yourself and others. The theme of connectedness is central to these guidelines.

41

1. BE OPEN TO YOUR AWARENESS.

"Personal transformation is part of evolution and the greatest gift we can give each other is the quality of our attention."[2]

Without awareness, you cannot see yourself or others with any degree of clarity. In other words, awareness means that you notice and think about what happens to you and your loved ones. It means that you notice what you feel as well as what you do with these feelings. Awareness involves fully experiencing your behavior, thinking, feeling, spirituality, and noticing any obstacles to your experiencing. From this awareness, you can then begin a process that enables you to know what is happening in the lives of your family.

Another word for this process is consciousness. Consciousness allows you to know all that is possible to know about yourself and others. There is no other way to understand yourself or your children. To whatever degree you consciously or unconsciously avoid awareness, you limit the knowledge you could obtain. You cannot use what you do not know. From my perspective, awareness and knowledge of your thinking, feeling, behavior, and spirituality will provide the resources to allow true change. Change stemming from your insides will be uniquely yours. This is quite different from being told to be or how to be different. This knowledge is the key to personal power, and this personal power is profoundly greater than any power that comes from your position in life.

Consciousness, then, means awareness: being conscious of yourself, conscious of others, and conscious of your environment. This consciousness can and will make a difference in your own world. It can make a real difference in the larger world as well. Our culture benefits when its members become aware of their own and others' needs. It benefits, too, when people choose healthy and balanced ways to fulfill these needs.

QUESTIONS TO ASK YOURSELF:

A. What happened today that I liked?
B. What happened today that I did not like?
C. What role did I play in these happenings?
D. What role did others play in these happenings?
E. What emotions were present in these happenings?
F. How did I experience and express these emotions?
G. How did each person influence the outcome of these happenings?
H. What concerns do I have about the world that influence my family?

POSSIBLE PITFALLS:

A. As you and your family members open yourselves, you may feel overwhelmed by the information and feelings; the feeling of being overwhelmed is a major reason for denial. It is important to give yourself and other family members encouragement as well as time to process their increasing awareness. Often this is referred to as giving space.

---

2. BE OPEN TO THE TRUTH.

"There is little prospect of getting rid of error except by the discovery of new truth."[3]

You cannot have awareness without openness to truth. There is an old saying that "the truth shall set you free." This powerful statement reflects two important points. Truth is a statement of reality. Without a statement of reality, you have no way of knowing what you are dealing with, and consequently, you cannot make appropriate decisions.

QUESTIONS TO ASK YOURSELF:

A. In what situations do I find it hard to accept things as they are?
B. What gets in the way of my accepting reality?
C. What do I do about accepting reality as it really is?
D. When am I overly tactful or in denial as a way of protecting others?
E. How do I go about getting affirmation of my reality?

POSSIBLE PITFALLS:

A. Being open to the truth may create discomfort in those who have a hard time accepting reality; especially if they have gone to great lengths to avoid reality.
B. As in guideline one, you may find yourself overwhelmed by the truth of your life. Please remember, you can use the truth to make constructive changes in your life.

3. BE OPEN TO ALL OF YOUR EXPERIENCE.

For both you and your child, experience is the great teacher in life. I am referring to the internal experience of yourself and your child. Earlier, I used the term "personal" to describe the internal perspective of individuals. It is very clear that people do not change or adopt differing values just because someone tells them to change. If an experience is not personal, people will look for external reasons for behaving a certain way. But once an experience is personal (internal), a person reacts to it as a part of her being. Reacting because it is part of a person's being is quite different from reacting for external reasons.

To understand your personal experience is to allow both you and your child to be in touch with an innermost part of being, the "core" of your being. This is where you really live your life. This core gives rise to your feelings. These feeling experiences are the source of your sense of aliveness. Therefore, you must feel in order to be really alive. Otherwise, you deaden yourself and contribute to the deadening of your children.

Another way of saying this is that you can numb yourself in the same way a dentist uses Novocaine to numb pain. The major problem with deadening the experience is that your mind and body have "recorded" the experience, and you carry the knowledge in your subconscious mind. This recorded information does influence you, but you do not know when or how it is influencing you. Numbing limits awareness.

The difference between what you permit in your awareness and what has been recorded in your subconscious can cause internal conflict. That is, one part of you knows something is there, and another part of you wants to forget. These parts are in conflict and will split you. This conflict and splitting could result in your feeling helpless, depressed, or most likely, anxious. Such feelings can be very mild or quite strong. In short, many people describe themselves as being unable to be all they feel they can be.

By being open to all of your experience you are more alive. There is great freedom in being more alive. The cost of this freedom is an awareness of events and behaviors you might prefer to forget. On consideration, the cost of forgetting is very high.

QUESTIONS TO ASK YOURSELF:

A. How alive do I feel?

B. Under what conditions do I feel myself constricted or anxious?

C. Do I sometimes have a sense of detachment as if I am watching life instead of being a part of it? If so, when?

D. When do I push myself or the children not to experience feelings that are or may be unpleasant?

POSSIBLE PITFALLS:

A. You may feel out of control until you learn to trust letting the experience just pass through.

B. Your experiencing may create discomfort in others.

C. The pain may seem like it is more than you can bear. If this is the case, you may have fears about going "crazy." Or you may fear being overwhelmed by the deeply felt emotions. These are typical fears. If you feel these intense fears, professional consultation is essential (please see Chapter 9). If you consider professional consultation, please be clear about the type of approach you desire.

---

4. BE OPEN TO ALL EMOTIONALITY.

Emotionality is often thought of as irrational, destructive, or both. Such thought is defensive and full of denial. This attitude toward emotions occurs when awareness, truthfulness, and experiencing are denied. By being open to the truth of your feelings, you can admit to how these feelings are experienced. Awareness shows you how your internal and external experiences relate. Through your truthfulness, you have awareness, which allows you to act rationally and choose nondestructive ways of expressing your feelings.

The destructive use of emotions has had a large impact on many individuals and on our culture—remember the boiled frog syndrome? As a result, we as a culture tend to hide our feelings and deaden ourselves. To me, this is a main contributor to addictions and many of our other societal ailments. I propose to you an alternative. Teach your children to express their feelings constructively so these feelings do not get "bottled-up." This is very important because emotions are the energies that pour out of life experiences. This flowing of energy creates the sensation that you are experiencing life. Without the flow of emotional energies; you deaden yourself; you will not fully experience life. To say this differently, feelings are the "fuel" for feeling alive. Without this fuel, most individuals will search for other fuel—the addictions that occur in our society. However, the bottom line is when you deaden or block your emotional experiences, you deaden your life experience. Deadening is the root of most emotional difficulties. These emotional difficulties can be devastating both for the person who is trying to deal with them and for caring others. We all need awareness, truthfulness, and emotionality to enable connectedness.

QUESTIONS TO ASK YOURSELF:

A. In general, what freedom do I have to feel anger, sadness, joyfulness (jumping-up and-down joyful), frustration, fear, disappointment, love, pride, confidence, and acceptance? In what situations do I feel free to experience each?

B. Which emotions do I avoid, and which emotions do I seek out?

C. How do I express each of these emotions?

D. What do I tell myself about feeling each of these emotions?

E. What emotions do I consider "strong," and what emotions do I consider "weak"?

F. When do others' emotions seem stronger than the situation would appear to warrant?

G. When are my emotions stronger than the situation warrants?

H. When do I let myself become overly influenced or controlled by another's feelings?

I. Do I return to a sense of calm after expressing my feelings, or do I "block" and continue to carry the emotional energy?

J. Am I in a constant state of tension or anxiety?

K. Do I wonder if I will ever really feel free and whole?

POSSIBLE PITFALLS:

A. You might become so emotional that you completely lose sight of how you affect others. This loss could destroy the balance between the fulfillment of your own needs and the needs of those you love.

B. Either you or others could use emotions as a way of manipulating.

C. You could become so emotional you lose track of what your mind is telling you. This could be destructive if you lose your sense of purpose or become excessively helpless. A balance or integration between your mind and emotions is possible. If you or a family member cannot do this on your own, please seek professional consultation.

5. BE OPEN TO AFFECTION AND LOVE.

I strongly believe the need for touch, affection, and love is a universal human need. For too many people, this need is accompanied by a feeling of being vulnerable and exposed. Some people even use the expression "wimpy" to describe their need for love and attention. Yet these same people are looking for something to fill their lives. On the one hand, they will deny that they desire love and attention; but on the other, they look for ways to fill this need. This attitude is very confusing, and one might even consider it a form of craziness. Difficulties in experiencing closeness are almost always learned in childhood.

It should not surprise you that your child will be affected by the intensity of love she receives from you. Your love gives your child a sense that it is OK to love herself. Another way of saying this is your love gives your child affirmation of her own love. In very practical terms, this gives your child a sense that she is loveable. If she does not feel loveable, she will experience some form (possibly mild to serious) of emotional difficulty. At the very least, she needs to feel loveable to feel whole. So, without the sense of loveability (love-ability), your child will be prone to feeling excessively vulnerable and exposed. I want to emphasize this point, since people who feel good about themselves in a deep and real way are more loving and considerate of others than those who feel badly about themselves. Feeling badly about yourself depletes your resources and takes away your sense of freedom, which then makes it difficult to be caring. Lovingness restores these resources and gives back the sense of freedom and wholeness.

This lovingness can be more difficult in hard or tragic times, but these times may be a source of coming together in a powerful way. And from this togetherness comes the power to overcome the hard time. Of course, in a hard time, there can be either a constructive sharing of deeply felt emotions or a sense of blaming to drive people apart. Blaming just creates defensiveness and distance. The sharing of deeply felt emotions creates a deeper sense of intimacy. During hard times, your task is to create a sharing of these deeply felt emotions so that your child knows you are with her. This knowledge provides a sense of two people being together in a tender, loving, sensitive way. This experience draws people together and therefore is the ultimate measure of loving.

QUESTIONS TO ASK YOURSELF:

A. In what ways do I express affection and love?

B. In what ways do I sense my own loveability (love-ability)?

C. Is it easier for me to love others than myself?

D. Do I withdraw love in times of stress? When was love withdrawn from me?

E. Does my deep-level loving remind me of times when loving was hurtful?

F. What did I learn about loving in my early childhood years?

POSSIBLE PITFALLS:

A. Some people "love" so much they live for their children instead of themselves. This is not good for you or your child. Continually putting your child's needs above your own gives your child entirely too much psychological power. This is a poor model of the "give and take" of healthy love!

B. Loving may stimulate fear when it reminds someone of extremely difficult childhood times. This can be so extreme that love and pain may feel the same to this individual. Under these circumstances, it would seem essential to "unravel" this connection, possibly with professional help. This help will also enable and support other family members to be more open and trusting.

C. Being open to love and affection does not mean confusing sexuality with loving. Loving is a whole process that includes the entire person being loved. Sexuality between an adult and child is not loving; it

---

is a physical, emotional, and psychological violation of the child's love and trust. This violation scars deeply. However, emotions are quite complicated, and there are possibilities that sexual feelings may arise in the middle of closeness. As always, feelings can be acted upon in either constructive or destructive ways. A child should not be involved with these sexual feelings. If you have reason to fear your sexual feelings, you can benefit from professional counseling. Through this help, you will not have to distance yourself, which would give your child the wrong impression. Distancing yourself could lead to her feeling conflicted about closeness and affection.

6. BE OPEN TO LIVING IN THE MOMENT.

Life occurs in the here and now. If you are constantly in the past or in the future, you will miss life's moments. Most importantly, you will miss the "magic" moments of your child as she grows. Living in the past or the future takes the life of the moment away. It is also likely to teach your child not to live in the moment. People who have a hard time living in the moment are likely to have problems with boredom and/or dissatisfaction. If you are one of these people, try to remember your early history. You may discover what event or series of events resulted in your loss of spontaneity. With this examination, you may find the resolution to living in the "here and now." Examining your personal history can be the first step in recovering your spontaneity.

QUESTIONS TO ASK YOURSELF:

A. How do I experience events as they happen to me? Can I be aware with all four basic parts?

B. Do I overly concentrate on thinking about events or do I just let myself be a part of what is happening in the moment?

C. Can I celebrate present moments?

D. Do I spend a lot of time projecting into the future?

E. Do I get upset over my child's spontaneity?

F. Can I enjoy activities just for the sake of enjoying them, or must there be a "higher" purpose?

G. What past events keep me from being in the moment?

H. Am I aware of moments that tend to put me in the past or the future?

I. Do I make large efforts to be "in control"?

POSSIBLE PITFALLS:

A. You could be so in the moment you never stop to think about past events that affect you now.

B. You could be so in the moment that you never stop to think about how your behavior will affect you in the future.

C. You could be so in the moment that you lose sight of how your behavior affects others. As a result, you could lose your sense of connectedness to others.

As always, living in the moment is <u>balanced</u> with understanding your past and future. This is a dynamic process that results from balancing your awareness of your past with your awareness of the present. With this balance and integration, you will have a more expansive, more fulfilling future made up of its own present-living moments. As you live in this moment and those to come, you are more likely to be full of spirit.

7. BE OPEN TO YOUR CHILDREN AS SEPARATE INDIVIDUALS.

Seeing your child as separate from you is a lot like walking a tightrope—it is difficult; it may even feel impossible. One side of the tightrope is seeing your child's point of view. The other side is seeing your child through your own eyes. Balancing these perspectives can be extremely complicated. There are three major reasons for the difficulty in recognizing separateness, and they often overlap: the intensity of the infant-parent bond, confusion of your childhood with your child's, and over-responsibility.

After birth, the infant-parent bond is so great that a parent usually identifies with all of the child's needs. Infants depend on this identification to develop a sense of basic trust. As your child matures, the parent-child bond continues, but it is tempered so that your child can experience life first-hand. With first-hand experiences, your child learns to be separate and whole while experiencing connectedness. If your parent-child bond remains too intense, you may overly identify with your child, and major difficulties can develop. Typically, these difficulties lead to a child who feels too powerful and controlling. She is then likely to feel a sense of unwanted responsibility and anger.

The second difficulty in recognizing separateness can come from confusing your own childhood with your child's. There is absolutely no doubt that your childhood affects the way you parent—usually in one of two ways. The first is that you can work very hard to create a different childhood for your child. With this choice, parents have a tendency to go to the extreme. The second choice is to parent the way you remember being raised. This is often a conscious choice and involves many repetitions of your childhood. With either choice, your parenting is based on your childhood experiences and not on the unique needs and separateness of your child. Let me give a quick example. If you were frightened of competition as a child, you might assume that your child is frightened of competition. From this position, you may be overly protective, or conversely, you might push for more competitiveness. Either approach ignores your child's having a voice in decisions that affect her.

The third difficulty in balancing separateness is **responsibility**. Many parents feel so responsible for their children that they make the same mistakes that result from the first two reasons (too intense bonding and confusion of parent's childhood). This intense sense of responsibility can come from three sources. One is the parent's history, which was covered above. The second is that parents do not want their children to make the same mistakes they made growing up. The third is that some parents fear that their children cannot handle the consequences of their mistakes. In this instance, parents are so responsible that their children never receive the consequences of their behavior. Instead, parents constantly rescue them, denying them a sense of full experience and competency.

There is another area that concerns me, although fortunately, progress has been made in some sectors of society. This is the area of what is considered masculine and what is considered feminine. If I had my "druthers," I would erase these words from society's vocabulary. These words often give people license to decide what boys should do and what girls should do. This is very limiting for a child of either gender. However, the words do occur, and there are some professionals who believe that labeling qualities as masculine or feminine can be helpful. If you will think about personality traits, it is obvious that each child carries a unique combination of traits. Your job is to help your child develop all of these traits in a balanced way. To do this, you will need to respect your child's unique combination of traits and affirm her development during all constructive interactions.

In summary, I hope it is clear that your child has a unique personality and is living a life different from yours. Knowing that you hold this vision, she can mature within limits that will allow for sensitivity to others. She will then remain connected.

QUESTIONS TO ASK YOURSELF:

A. How is my child different from me?

B. What makes my child different from other children?

C. How is my child similar to other children?

D. Do I see my child as a reflection of me so that I have difficulty letting her make mistakes from which she could learn?

E. Can I look at my child and see how special he or she is?

F. Do I categorize behaviors into feminine and masculine so that certain behaviors are highly discouraged or ignored?

POSSIBLE PITFALLS:

A. Your sense of your child's uniqueness might lead you to be overly permissive and not encourage a balanced adaptation to the requirements of the world. Children need limits to learn a realistic sense of their limitations. Both too few and too many limits can be psychological killers. I have yet to read the "right" amount of limits for a child. Your sensitivity, if adequately developed, can provide you with your own basic answer to this question.

B. You could possibly be so overwhelmed by her separateness that you become emotionally distant in your everyday living. Your sense of her separateness is not meant to create distance but to recognize, support, and love her individuality and uniqueness. This will have a profound effect on her self-esteem.

---

8. BE OPEN TO CHANGE.

As you well know, your life has been one of constant change since you were a small child. Depending on a variety of circumstances, these changes have been either easy or difficult for you. Remembering the nature of these changes can help you prepare for the many changes that are ahead for your child.

For some people, being open to change is not easy. Typically, the reluctance to change arises from comfort with the familiar and fear of what might happen if things do change; fear of uncertainty and the unknown. It is extremely interesting to notice how many people will not change a "bad" situation because they have become accustomed to it. This is complicated by the fact that these people "know what to do" in the bad situation, and they are used to dealing with it. Consequently, many people believe and act as if they are unable to change.

Another form of resistance to change is not knowing the "right thing to do." As human beings, we often do not know the "right" thing, and we fear the risk of being wrong. However, if you examine and "tune into" your values and your feelings, you will find the strength to change. You will also find yourself much stronger through struggling with your deepest values and feelings.

Being open to change involves being open to risks. This may scare you, and many of the risks are indeed scary. But you cannot go into a cave and sleep the rest of your life away. There is the risk of trusting your child more than you were trusted as a child. There is also the risk of not trusting your child. Finally, there is the risk of being vulnerable to love and pain. Without accepting these risks, your life is likely to become either very dead or very destructive.

QUESTIONS TO ASK YOURSELF:

A. What phases of my life were the easiest?

B. What phases of my life were the most difficult?

C. How did I cope with these changes, and what did I learn about change?

D. How has life changed since the birth of my child?

E. What changes do I foresee in the future of my child?

F. Am I open to changes that come naturally with the increasing age of my child?

G. As my child is ready, am I willing to let my child make mistakes and suffer the consequences?

H. Am I willing to take risks when I am not quite sure of the proper thing to do?

I. Do I find myself being overly protective of my children?

POSSIBLE PITFALLS:

A. You could be so open to change that you resist your child's remaining in a particular developmental phase. There will be signs suggesting time for movement into the next developmental phase.

B. You could be so open to change that there is no consistent theme to either your sense of direction or your communication. Your child needs some degree of consistency but not so much that you are rigid. As an aware parent you will balance openness with boundaries.

---

9. BE OPEN TO VERBAL AND NONVERBAL COMMUNICATION.

It goes without saying communication is the vehicle for interacting with other people. These interactions are maintained in their purest form when the communication is **direct** and clearly reflects the message to be delivered. Communication provides your child a vehicle for learning, a way of relating to the family, and a model for communicating outside the family. Communication is the expression of your thoughts and feelings. Inner communication is listening carefully to all of your thoughts and feelings. Without inner communication, neither you nor your child have an inner "voice." Your inner voice more fully extends communication and intimacy.

I would like to highlight four major qualities of positive communication: 1. your outward words (the words that others hear) reflect the truth of what you are saying to yourself with inner words (the words that no one else can hear); 2. your inner words reflect your own personal truth to the best of your ability; 3. you have some sense of your listener so you can choose words appropriate to the occasion; 4. your words are respectful of the other person as a human being.

With awareness of these four qualities, you can communicate much more effectively. Good communication between your inner and your outer self is essential.

QUESTIONS TO ASK YOURSELF:

A. When am I hesitant to say what I think and feel?

B. Am I able to communicate my innermost thoughts and feelings effectively?

C. What topics are the most uncomfortable for me? What topics are taboo?

D. When am I not open to hearing the messages of others?

E. Do I hear changes in speech such as volume, speed, and emotion?

F. Am I able to perceive the meaning of facial expressions?

G. Am I comfortable in looking at others and establishing eye contact?

H. Am I aware of my body posture and physical distance from others?

I. When do I or other people choose words for their power to manipulate?

J. Do I choose excessively critical communication?

K. Do I use communication to help others choose?

L. Do I listen in order to criticize or judge?

M. Am I likely to get defensive or to attack when listening to others?

N. When praising others, do I mix in negative criticism?

O. Am I able to give criticism in respectful and constructive ways?

POSSIBLE PITFALLS:

A. Communication, when it is for the sake of communication, does just that—relates a message. Therefore, with the exception of destructive messages, my sense is that there are no pitfalls. This does not mean everyone will be happy with what is communicated. There will be disagreements and misinterpretations. In other words, people will not always "get it." As you are secure with yourself, you will expect and accept disagreements and misinterpretations. Your security will lead you to communicate further and resolve disagreements and misunderstandings. If you are secure in this expectation, you are not as likely to be "thrown off" by typical communication difficulties. You may then refine your message.

10. BE OPEN TO YOUR EXPECTATIONS.

Expectations are powerful psychological experiences. First, they can strongly influence the way you perceive certain events. For example, if you expect your child to obtain "A"s in school, you will react quite differently to her "C"s than if you were expecting "C"s. Second, expectations can create what are called "self-fulfilling prophesies." This phrase describes the power of expectations, whether conscious or unconscious, to contribute to their realization. For example, if you have "struck-out" a number of times, it is only natural for you to expect to "strike-out" again. Or, for example, fearing that your child will get into deep trouble can give her encouragement or even "permission" to get into trouble. Your expectation is perceived by her as a message upon which she acts. Most of the time, this permission is given without awareness, but the results are still the same—"trouble."

As you deal with this trouble, you may become more aware of your expectations—of yourself and your child. Please be careful about how you handle both the conscious and unconscious intentions of your child. The bottom line is simple: if you expect positive outcomes and behave in a way that goes with your positive expectations, you are much more likely to receive positive results.

As you can see, expectations play an important role in your life. Expectations are natural to the condition of being human and occur as a result of all that has happened to you. If you are conscious of expectations, you can make decisions to break free of those that are not in your best interest. It would be of value to discuss your expectations with an objective friend or a professional.

61

QUESTIONS TO ASK YOURSELF:

A. What do I expect of my child?

B. Which events contribute to my expectations? What childhood events led to my expectations of adulthood?

C. When is my expectation so strong it is likely to influence the outcome of a situation—in other words, a self-fulfilling prophecy?

D. What do I do with my fearful expectations?

E. Do I expect feelings and behaviors that are beyond my child's capabilities?

F. Am I excessively moralistic and judgmental?

G. Am I open to the imperfections in my children?

H. Do I openly expect my child to provide reasonable challenges to my authority as a way of her asserting a separate sense of identity?

I. Do my expectations allow my child to have a feeling of choice?

J. Do I allow for moments of celebration before moving on to the next challenge?

POSSIBLE PITFALLS:

A. In looking at your expectations you could go too far and eliminate those expectations that help you and others to change and grow. If this should happen, you are likely to become overly permissive and not expect enough to stimulate and support the growth of your child.

---

11. BE OPEN TO SETTING LIMITS.

There are many ideas relating to how people can live together in a peaceful, harmonious way. A part of me believes that with greater levels of love, freedom, respect, and self-esteem, people could live together harmoniously. The realistic part of me knows that these levels have not yet been achieved, nor am I sure they will ever be. There appears to be a need for rules and limits. However, rules and limits require balance with the need for love, freedom, respect, and self-esteem.

With this balance, there might be less resentfulness of authority. There would be a greater emphasis on positive limit setting, resulting in more mutual and positive relationships. Within your own family, I would hope that the mutual sharing of love and freedom would outweigh the need for rules and limits. When relationships are truly caring, the need for rules is minimal; each person respects the others' limits. The optimal way would be the way of balance.

Finding and maintaining balance between freedom and limits is a very difficult task, and yet a very important one. Balance requires constant monitoring. On the one hand, you want your child to experience the love and freedom involved in being comfortable with herself. On the other hand, you recognize that being herself **can** be hurtful to others. She needs to understand, accept, and grow from her hurtful behavior. As you fully understand this, you assist in growth that enhances self-esteem.

You can help by telling her how her hurtful behavior feels to you. Also, she can learn through consequences in accordance with her hurtful behavior. These forms of feedback can focus on the behavior in question and not on the personality of your child. Your feedback can balance criticism with a sense of respect and understanding. Messages of respect and understanding serve as messages to be absorbed and to model how your child can treat others. You are not trying to make a robot of your child. Hopefully, your example will teach her to balance her own needs with the needs of others.

A positive image of this balance is that of a container, with the container being the limit. Within the container, your child may do as she pleases. Within the container, your child has lots of room to move around and grow. This gives her a sense of freedom and a sense of safety. Once your child moves beyond the edge of the container, she will have "fallen out," in a manner of speaking. In other words, she will have "crossed the line" set by the limits. As she learns to recognize the edge of the container and beyond, she will come to realize that freedom has an outer limit called responsibility. With responsibility, there are also consequences. I believe your task is to allow the experience of feeling these consequences, so she may incorporate the feelings as a part of herself. She may then incorporate the freedom that she experiences, as well as the hurtfulness of freedom taken too far. This is the balance between sensitivity to oneself and sensitivity to others. The image of the container comes from Albert Pesso (a noted therapist and founder of Psychomotor Therapy), and it is very useful in teaching both a sense of freedom and a sense of personal boundaries. This balance is certainly a needed virtue in this society.

QUESTIONS TO ASK YOURSELF:

A. What limits have I set in the past?

B. What limits do I intend to set in the future?

C. What atmosphere have I used to carry out these limits?

D. What messages are received in the way I carry out limits?

E. Do I confuse punishment with discipline and teaching?

F. Am I respectful of my child's character as limits are being set?

G. What are my feelings when my limits are challenged?

H. How were limits set when I was a child?

I. How does my child respond when the limits are clear and consistent?

J. How does my child respond when the limits are vague and inconsistent?

K. Does my limit-setting allow my child to learn from her own mistakes?

L. In what ways do I attempt to acknowledge and respect the feelings of my child when she is upset with the limits?

M. Do I let myself be manipulated by my child's feelings?

POSSIBLE PITFALLS:

A. It is possible to use limits primarily for your own convenience and not for the welfare of your child.

B. It is possible to use limits as a way of expressing feelings about situations unfinished from your own childhood.

C. It is possible for you to be overly sensitive and give your child the power of an adult. Children are in the process of growing into adults. It is said, "You are working yourself out of a job." If you set limits with love and respect, you will not work yourself out of a long lasting relationship with remarkable potential.

12. BE OPEN TO MISTAKES.

Children are not perfect, and for that matter, neither are we adults. Many parents are not aware of their perfectionistic attitudes and how they teach this. Some parents openly acknowledge striving for perfection. Perfection is an unreasonable goal and comes with a high price. Typically, this price is frustration, excessive anger, lowering of self-esteem, and a feeling of being "horrible." As you think about the consequences of perfectionism, you will see its destructive side. An alternative view is teaching attainable expectations. This simply means that your expectations would be compatible with your child's abilities. This teaching emphasizes improving and learning from past behavior; it is a way of growth.

The goal of looking at mistakes is the goal of balance. On the one side of balance is the sense of forgiveness. From the side of forgiveness, you can be loving and generous as you help your child learn from her mistakes. This gives permission for loving growth. On the other side of balance, you can reduce the frequency of unwanted behaviors and eliminate those that are clearly detrimental. In dealing lovingly with unwanted behaviors, you may allow your child enough humanness to be imperfect. In this vein, I hope you **could** be pleased with a dramatic reduction in the frequency of these unwanted behaviors. There will always be unwanted behaviors, and, unless you accept this, you are likely to have a very negative attitude.

As you consider your openness to mistakes, I would like you to consider contradictory messages of forgiveness within society. On some occasions, you will find messages of love and forgiveness, and, on others, you will find messages of harshness and hate. Cultural harshness and hatred do not lead to forgiveness or a sense of loving and cannot be allowed to filter into the family. Of course, there are personal violations leading to hatred, and hopefully, these feelings can be resolved. I am advocating a balance that rejects excessive anger, harshness, or hatred. I do not believe you want your children to absorb harshness and hatred into their personalities. Harsh criticism only encourages mistakes and psychological blindness, blindness to love and openness.

I strongly urge you to monitor your attitudes toward mistakes. With increased awareness, you can reduce the frequency of your child's unwanted behaviors and "mistakes." You can also give her a sense of your loving presence as she learns and profits from experience. If you are successful, your children will not be excessively angry, punitive, withdrawn, depressed, or destructive. Through your loving attempts to teach, your child can be more loving of herself and others.

QUESTIONS TO ASK YOURSELF:

A. How do I react to my own sense of mistakes?
B. Do I let mistakes strongly influence my sense of self-worth?
C. Do I overreact to mistakes made by my children?
D. Do I resort to name-calling when mistakes occur?
E. Can I forgive myself and others when there are mistakes that are not intentional or abusive?
F. Can I see that reducing the number of mistakes is more important than obtaining perfection?
G. Do I view mistakes as opportunities to learn?
H. Am I able to see both the positive as well as the negative side of most events?
I. How hard do I work at being the "good" or "perfect" parent?
J. Do I constantly remind my children of their mistakes?
K. How easy is it for me to accept that I might be "wrong"?

POSSIBLE PITFALLS:

A. You may become so lenient that your child does not learn from her mistakes. In the real world there are consequences; sometimes there is punishment. Your child needs to learn how different consequences and punishment feel.
B. There are people that "use" mistakes as a way of changing or avoiding responsibility. These individu-

---

als will continue to repeat the mistake with an accompanying "I'm sorry." When the effort to change is not apparent, you can easily tell when someone is trying to manipulate you. **It has been said that the most sincere apology is an attempt at changing one's behavior.** I believe this to be true.

I would like to end this section with a quote:

"**If I can find someone who forgives, that is, refuses to be embittered and estranged, someone, who, bearing the effects of my sin, loves me still; then the power of that appeal is, I think, to all normal people—and I would venture to say in the last resort to all human beings — IRRESISTIBLE.**" [4]

This quote is quite powerful, and I recommend thinking about it in a very careful way.

13. BE OPEN TO OTHER'S VIEWS.

We human beings have many "blind spots" that keep us from seeing all aspects of any particular situation. Each of us has our habitual ways of seeing things, and from this perspective we can miss information needed for decision-making. I would hope you would appreciate that the world is full of opinions, and a great deal of the world is neither pure "black or white." Consequently, if you are going to understand the opinions of others, you must listen very carefully. You can absorb what is important to you and consider the rest. This is very important in listening to your children. Your children can often bring a new light to a variety of situations. **You can learn a great deal about truth, freedom, and emotionality from your children.**

A major stumbling block for being open to others' views is risk: you might regret what you hear, you might feel wrong, or you might make the wrong decision. Avoiding risks does not eliminate risk or their reality. Life, in many ways, is uncontrollable! Many people preach that you can control life, but this is an illusion. You can only control your own behavior. As a result, it is important that you play the odds of life in the best manner possible. You may do this by being open to a variety of views and opinions. In reality, there is no other choice; because each parent and child combination is different, there is no set of "right" answers. There are many loving, guiding principles. By listening and discussing with others, you can gain a variety of views that might be helpful in your quest for making parental decisions. Talking with others will comfort you with the knowledge of not being alone in your questions and concerns.

QUESTIONS TO ASK YOURSELF:

A. How open are you to others' opinions?

B. Do you overreact emotionally to others' opinions?

C. Do you get defensive in a discussion where there are contrasting opinions?

D. Do you try to make situations seem black or white without seeing the grays?

E. What is your openness to taking risks?

F. Are you open to learning from your children's thoughts, feelings, and behaviors? They can bring fresh meaning to old subjects.

POSSIBLE PITFALLS:

A. You can go too far in your willingness to listen and, as a result, let people overwhelm or manipulate you.

B. You could become so willing to listen, you lose your ability to be assertive.

C. You could become so willing to listen, you could lose your sense of identity.

---

14. BE OPEN TO FIGHTING.

Fighting is a rather controversial subject in psychology. Some people argue that fighting is OK; some argue it is part of being alive; and some argue it is destructive. In order to maintain your integrity and dignity, there are times when you must fight. This is not the kind of fighting that has the intent to destroy someone, but the kind of fighting in which you and your children stand your ground for what you believe. It is important that your children learn the difference.

They can develop the personal strength, self-esteem, and self-confidence to stand up for their rights, defend their position, and give a clear "NO" to destructive forces. Saying "NO" can come from either a sense of personal power or rebelliousness. Hopefully, you and your child can collaborate when you are not sure.

Being able to say "no" comes from establishing and maintaining a balanced sense of separate and connected identity. This takes collaborative practice. While hearing "no" from our children is often thought of as a rebellious challenge (and sometimes it is), it is most often an assertion of separateness. In openness, this serves as an opportunity for collaboration. Clearly, you are mistaken if you think your children will not try to establish their own boundaries. While initially this may seem bad to you, it is these boundaries that will allow your child to say no to drugs, unethical behavior, and immorality.

While fighting may begin as an assertion of separateness that needs to be dealt with in an open-minded way, the real key to resolving family fights is in what occurs during and following the fight. Within the fight, the interaction needs to be respectful of the other person's dignity, and the fight should not be an attempt to "destroy" the other person. The fight can be heated and intense without being disrespectful. After the fight, there can be a discussion of the reasons and feelings that occurred in the fight. This discussion can lead to collaboration. This can be accomplished through brainstorming, listing choices, and discussing priorities with a spirit of cooperation. From this cooperative interaction, the difficulty can usually be resolved without outside consultation.

QUESTIONS TO ASK YOURSELF:

A. Do I consider fighting as extremely negative?
B. Can I maintain my sense of identity in a fight?
C. Am I aware when the fighting has turned "dirty"?
D. How easy is it to say or hear the word "no"?
E. Can I maintain my position when someone is trying to manipulate me in a negative direction?
F. What kinds of feelings occur inside of me during a fight? How do I deal with these feelings?
G. Can I see a fight as an opportunity to cooperate?
H. Can I see both sides of an argument while in the middle of a fight?

POSSIBLE PITFALLS:

A. Fighting can become an exclusive way of life without the balance of love, giving, and forgiveness.
B. Fighting without considering the other person is usually destructive. Fighting can occur in a fair fashion.
NOTE: I am not endorsing physical fighting in any way, shape, or form.

---

15. BE OPEN TO THE MEANING OF MONEY.

Money is society's medium of exchange, and, as a result, serves a real purpose within the family. However, money can and often does take on powerful symbolic value. For example, money can be a substitute for a difficult childhood or broken dreams. It then becomes a measure of one's self-worth. Sometimes money is used to control or manipulate.

In the proper context, money is an asset to the family and can be used as an aspect of family discussions about vacations, toys, and other purchases relevant to your child. These discussions, like allowances, allow your child first-hand experience related to your money values, including buying versus saving, and instant versus delayed gratification. Money needs to be used for family purchases in a fair and balanced way.

QUESTIONS TO ASK YOURSELF:

A. Do I use money to satisfy my internal emotional needs?

B. Does there seem to be an excessive drive to continuously make more and more money?

C. Is money so valued in my family that it has more importance than emotional relationships?

D. At what point is my family satisfied with material wealth?

E. Is money used to control family behavior? If so, under what circumstances?

F. Are my children included in some of the decisions (appropriate to their age) concerning decorating needs, family toys, vacations, and so on?

POSSIBLE PITFALLS:

A. Children may get the message that they have control over money decisions by being included in discussions. It should be made clear that their input is highly valued, but that the final decision on purchases is yours.

B. Some individuals can become so careful about money that basic needs of family members are not met. This is dangerous to the person whose needs are not being met. Balance can be achieved as you discuss the definition of needs.

16. BE OPEN TO BEING SELFISH.

This idea tends to stir some vigorous controversy. Usually, we are taught to be generous and consider others first. While teaching generosity is a great idea in theory, two things can happen when it is taken to an extreme. The first is that you can be "run over" and become a "welcome mat" for others to use. The second is that many people use this idea of "doing good for others" as a way of taking care of themselves. In other words, one person can control another in the name of "doing what is good for you." However, this so-called good may be detrimental. A common way of saying this is, "The road to hell is paved with good intentions." For example, a parent who constantly emphasizes the future is unconsciously taking away their child's freedom to be spontaneous. Another example is the husband who works excessive hours "to make a better life" for the family and does not realize the devastating effect on the family. He probably will not admit to his excessive investment in his career.

Again, the important word here is balance: a balance between your own needs and the needs of others. **If you deplete yourself in giving to others, you will have little left to give.** You must be able to receive as well as give in order not to feel bitter, resentful, and used. At times, you will need to be selfish and serve your needs first. Be careful of those who are convinced that they know what is best for you. Be careful if you are always convinced that you know what is best for your child. A reasonable amount of questioning and consciousness will help both of you.

QUESTIONS TO ASK YOURSELF:

A. When do I let the needs of others take priority over my own needs?
B. What do I feel when someone is taking advantage of me?
C. When do I realize that others are taking unfair advantage of me?
D. When do I take care of my needs in a balanced way?
E. When am I clear about taking care of my own needs without becoming defensive?
F. Am I able to accept material and psychological gifts without guilt or embarrassment?

POSSIBLE PITFALLS:

A. You could become excessively selfish and not care in a meaningful way about others.

B. You could become so discouraged by the conflicts in the family that you put everyone else's needs before your own. You could do this by placating or by mediating all potential conflicts.

17. BE OPEN TO YOUR APPROACH TO PROBLEMS.

There are many styles of handling problems. Some are useful and others are not. These questions will help you discover your own style of approach.

QUESTIONS TO ASK YOURSELF:

A. Do I become excessively upset over facing problems?
B. Do I blame others or do I look for ways to resolve problems within myself?
C. Which types of problems are the most upsetting?
D. Which types of problems are the least upsetting?
E. Do I belittle or ignore problems?
F. Do I pay attention to the feelings that go with the problem?
G. Do I explore what contributes to these feelings?
H. Do I "drown" in the feelings to the point that I become helpless?
I. Can I let feelings of helplessness "push" me to take action?
J. Do I recognize when I literally have no control and am helpless to either change or stop something?
K. Can I step back and analyze my problems objectively?
L. Can I then formulate and proceed with a plan to solve my problem?
M. Do I make big deals out of trivial problems?

POSSIBLE PITFALLS:

A. You could try to be controlling when you really do not have control.
B. You could try to control situations you should not be controlling.
C. You could move to a place of helplessness and not take any action whatsoever.

---

18. BE OPEN TO YOUR STYLE OF PARENTING.

There are many varieties and styles of parenting. The three most frequently mentioned styles are authoritarian, democratic, and passive. Authoritarian means that parents are the "bosses" and children have little input into decisions. Democratic means that everyone has a say in the decisions, possibly an equal vote, depending on the family. Passive means that parents allow the children to have control, and they primarily follow the decisions of the children. Most parents have a blend of the three styles, depending on the situation. It would seem to me that a blend of the three with an emphasis on democracy is most appropriate. However, I would not expect you to be democratic in decisions where there is potential danger for your child. Last, but not least, the final blend of these styles will be determined by the **needs** and **abilities** of your children.

QUESTIONS TO ASK YOURSELF:

A. Under what circumstances am I very controlling?

B. Do I use power in such a way that there are too many power struggles?

C. Do I parent in such a way that the needs of the family are balanced?

D. Does everyone in the family have an opportunity to speak of their needs?

E. How protective am I?

F. Do I encourage an excessive amount of dependence or independence?

G. Do I consider my parenting style democratic, passive, or authoritarian?

19. BE OPEN TO YOUR PAST.

"I can't look through the eyes of a younger me because the glass of my perception is made up of experiences and memories." [5]

"No man, be he lawyer, doctor, priest or poet, can correctly describe the real history of another . . . The little events that determine the growth of the soul, the secret memories that colour his mentality, the hidden springs from which arise his motives and his actions, these no friend, however intimate, can fully know." [6]

"For the sake of my future and its possible significance, I must remember what the past has brought me; I *know* only what I have experienced, and I must remember what I *know*." [7]

These statements are another confirmation of my own belief that my past is a part of my present and my future. My history can, and often does, play a powerful role in influencing what I think and what I feel. This does not mean that I am bound by my past; I am free to understand my past and make decisions in the here and now. Hence, I can be much more aware of my intentions and behavior. You and every other human being have a history. I believe it borders on the tragic to minimize the importance of history. **Every moment of your life becomes your history—as soon as the moment passes.** This thought is enlivening.

Many people have argued that since you cannot change the past, "Why think about it?" While they are correct about not being able to change their past, they are avoiding how their past experiences may be affecting them. In making decisions you need the full information that your history provides. **Remembering the pain of the past can be very helpful in not repeating it.**

To be unaware of your past, you must push memories into the subconscious, or out of awareness. This often occurs with people who carry the burden of a painful history and do not want to remember the pain. While I certainly can understand their wanting to forget, their memories are usually not far away from awareness. More importantly, these painful memories have greater power to control your behavior when they are not in your awareness. It is amazing how many people repeat negative or destructive experiences. In truly remembering the pain of the past, there is strong incentive not to re-create this pain in the present. Very few people would repeat this suffering consciously.

Last, but not least, looking at and feeling the memories of your past can provide you with a sense of freedom and energy. Keeping your memories hidden from your awareness cuts your sense of freedom to feel what occurs inside of you. This blocks your sense of experiencing. Looking at and feeling your past is not to blame or make excuses, it is for living. **If you are not using energy to block your experiencing, you then have greater amounts of energy to pour into living.**

Recovering your past gives you freedom and energy; recovering your past lowers the possiblility of repeating past mistakes. This will help you to understand how you came to be the way you are. To do this, I highly recommend a safe and supportive place (e.g. counseling environment, trusted friend) so that you will be encouraged to take the journey into your past.

QUESTIONS TO ASK YOURSELF:

A. What past events stand out in my memory?

B. Do I have periods of my history where I remember very little?

C. When do I have emotional reactions that are out of proportion to the situation?

D. What did I learn in my childhood that affects my parenting behavior?

E. What are the the strongest "do's" and "don't's" that I learned in my childhood?

F. What are the strongest "should's" and "should not's" from my childhood?

G. What are the strongest "can's" and "cannot's" from my childhood?
H. What do my children do that reminds me of my childhood?
I. What did I learn about expressing emotionality in my childhood?
J. What did I learn about expressing sensuality in my childhood?
K. What and how did I learn about sexuality in my childhood?
L. Do I have words and behaviors that just suddenly appear as if they came from nowhere?
M.What do I remember about my birthdays?
N. What do I remember about Christmas or other religious times?
O. What do I remember about pets in my childhood?
P. What do I remember about fears and excitements?
Q. What did I learn about guilt?

POSSIBLE PITFALLS:

A. In recovering past memories, you may experience psychological pain that is quite intense. It is my sense that you carry this pain, even if you try to keep it in the back of your mind. However, if you are not used to experiencing and letting pain "pass through," it could create problems. If you anticipate difficulties in experiencing your pain, I would suggest you obtain professional consultation to provide you with a guided, safe, and supportive atmosphere.

B. You could spend so much time thinking about the past that you essentially live in the past. However, if you use your history effectively, this is unlikely to happen. Instead, your inner and outer selves can flow freely, giving you energy for life and the freedom to love.

---

20. BE OPEN TO DEATH.

> **Because I can no longer ignore death,**
> **I pay more attention to life.**[8]

Death is often seen as a passage to a greater state of being. There are many who do not carry this belief. The fact of the matter is that we are all going to die. This does not have to be a morbid thought, but a realization that our days are limited and precious. It has been said that in order to fully experience our lives we must understand they will one day end. In one of Carlos Castaneda's books, Don Juan implored Castaneda to live life as though death were looking over his left shoulder. Hopefully, this knowledge will give you more energy and awareness in the living of your life. You can live life more fully as you encounter this difficult but freeing path of openness to death.

QUESTIONS TO ASK OF YOURSELF:

A. How have I reacted to the death of others?

B. What are my thoughts and feelings about the death of others?

C. What are my thoughts and feelings about my own death?

D. How have I presented death to my children? How did they respond?

E. If I were given one year to live, how would I live my life differently?

F. If my child were given one year to live, would I treat my child differently?

POSSIBLE PITFALLS:

A. You could become so obsessed with death that it interferes with living.

B. In the event of a death, you could become so involved that you do not recover after a reasonable period of time. If this should happen or if you become excessively depressed, please consult a professional therapist.

Chapter 4

ESTABLISHING A POSITIVE RELATIONSHIP
WITH YOUR CHILD

A positive relationship serves as the foundation for you to establish a connected relationship. Utilizing my training and experience, I have accumulated many ideas to establish a more positive relationship with your child. Some of these ideas may seem obvious, and others may not have occurred to you. Either way, it can be difficult to remember these ideas when you are overly focused on goals or when there is stress. Your good intentions to positively relate can easily be forgotten. Taking a few minutes each day to think about how you felt, thought, and behaved will help you focus and be more aware. Eventually, this practice will become very important to your sense of intimacy and connectedness.

I believe that expanding your parental relationship is of the utmost importance for four major reasons:

✓ 1. Your relationship will reflect the quality of the time that is spent together.
✓ 2. Conflicts will be easier to resolve.
✓ 3. This concentration enlivens the parenting experience.
✓ 4. Your relationship will serve as a model for your child's parenting.

The following are guidelines for establishing a positive life-long relationship with your child:

84

1. ALLOW YOURSELF TO GIVE DEEP LEVELS OF LOVE AND ATTENTION.

For many reasons families have a strong tendency to lose sight of the more meaningful aspects of life. It may be because there's not enough time or because some deadline must be met. When this happens, you are distracted from "being with" your child. Allow yourself to leave other concerns behind and focus on your "insides." Attempt to regain your aliveness and re-connect from your heart. You may then connect with your many feelings of deep love and tenderness.

Be obvious with both your enjoyment and your loving. Be obvious with your appreciation of being together. It does not hurt to say, "I'm glad we are together" or "I sure appreciate you." Please be open to share the joy that results from her presence, development, and companionship. I encourage you to say "I love you" and not assume that she knows. Please take time to be physically affectionate with non-sexual touching. Every child needs to learn that she deserves to be touched, and that she will not be harmed by those she loves. This balance teaches children non-sexual touching so they will readily know the difference later in life.

Encourage your child to discuss her daily concerns and, even when they seem minor to you, listen with the knowledge that these concerns are very important to her. Be strong in your conviction to learn as much as you can about your child. Be present at her activities and encourage her to enjoy the activities for the sake of relationship. When possible, participate in these activities yourself. Try to keep competitiveness in balance. As you spend quality time with your child, you will have the opportunity for many moments of sharing.

I would like to say something more about love. Love, as you well know, is a feeling that comes from the heart. When love exists in its truest sense, it does not expect a reward. This is usually referred to as unconditional love. In this sense, love is a connection between your soul and your child's soul. Love is an openness to receive your child's love; her gift of aliveness.

Through your own experience of having been a child, you

85

may have found your expressions of love either frustrated or accompanied by a great deal of pain. If this has happened, openness may be difficult and being with your child may remind you of your own painful experiences. Love and pain may then feel the same. If this is true for you, do your best to separate your childhood experiences from the experiences of your child.

Loving your child through the thick and thin of all experiences is the greatest affirmation of her being. Loving through both pain and joy is unconditional love. Loving can give your child the greatest affirmation of her internal processes. Unconditional love is what she needs to learn to be OK with being herself. Loving affirmation gives her permission to live moment to moment for the remainder of her life. Without affirmation, she will likely search for accomplishments and relationships to provide this permission. While these can enhance who she is, they will not give her permission to just "be."

Note: Unconditional love does not suggest being permissive or rigid in your parenting behavior.

2. REMEMBER THAT YOUR CHILD IS IN A PROCESS OF DEVELOPMENT.

Children go through a variety of developmental phases as they age. They are developing physically, emotionally, intellectually, and spiritually. Your child develops at different rates under different circumstances—at times you may become easily frustrated. It is all too easy to focus on a goal and leave out the process of achieving the goal. The process can either injure or enhance your child's self-esteem.

To enhance the possiblity of success and to ensure a higher level of self-esteem, I would like you to consider the steps (aspects) of whatever you are trying to encourage. Then, I would like you to consider how to order these steps for maximum progress. Finally, I would like for you to emphasize factual observations as feedback. Factual observations minimize the effects of excessive sensitivity to parental reactions.

Factual observations provide emphasis on positive development. As a result, little emphasis is put on the negative; including whether she is good or bad. For example, it is more positive to say, "It's nine o'clock" (with that bedtime hour being previously agreed upon) than to say, "You have been watching entirely too much TV." As another example, you might tell her that she tied her shoes three of five days rather than speaking to the other two days. It is not necessary to call her a "good" or a "bad" girl in response to her behavior. The use of "good" and "bad" girl confuses love, self-esteem, and achievement. In other words, these phrases often lead to negative self-appraisals.

Since you are interested in her progress and development, it will be tempting to overly praise when you are especially pleased with her progress. "Overly" means too much and can easily affect her self-esteem. Balanced praise is OK when it does not overly involve your child's self-esteem. Of course, you will not always approve of her behavior, and you will not always be focused on factual feedback.

Focus on forward movement in development and downplay failures. If your child is overreactive to failures, assure her that you are there to help her get through her struggle. Let her know how she can move through the struggle with your assistance. Assure her that you will work with her so that she will find her way to resolution.

These particular guidelines are rather broad, and I would like to give you a few concrete examples. First of all, let's consider a child who is learning to concentrate, slow down, and be more focused. First, you would consider the aspects of what you are trying to encourage. For me, concentration, slowing down, and being more focused means using one's mind, thinking slowly, and deliberately attending to one task. With this in mind, your child might be given a task where she has to count objects to determine the number of objects. If she is young, she may point to each one with your help as she counts. You might count along with her. Or to accomplish the same goal if she is older, you might ask her to listen to a story and give you feedback as you read to her. If she has difficulty, you can give her a repetition of the information she has not absorbed. If she continues to have difficulty, you might present examples of the feedback that she might later offer as a response.

If you are interested in how a child relates to people, you would think about the aspects of how a person generally does this. With this in mind, you might share with her that she appeared to remember that there were people talking and listening to her. Also, that she was talking and listening to others without interrupting them. These aspects or steps show how to be polite and respectful. If you are trying to encourage helpfulness, you might say "It was really helpful to the family that you picked up the dishes and took them to the sink."

Notice that these phrases reflect the aspects required for the task, and, at the same time, encourage an interaction between or among people. Notice that you are choosing phrases that increase sensitivity to the relationship. This increases **consciousness** of the relationship while she learns and develops.

Part of your job is to know as much as possible about your child's developmental phases and to recognize how these years offer her a basis for developing self-sufficiency. As your child matures, you will both make mistakes that present opportunities for learning. **If you resist the natural tendency to rescue or control**, you both can recover from mistakes and proceed further with her development of self-sufficiency. You can continue to be available nearby with encouragement. The bottom line is to attend more to the **process** of development while keeping the goals close behind. Without experiencing the process, the goal is meaningless. Without experiencing the process, we all lose aliveness and risk a sense of boredom. As you accomplish this, she can see you as a helpful, loving teacher who models respectful, loving interactions.

3. REMEMBER THAT CHILDREN ARE EXTREMELY SENSITIVE AND QUITE AWARE.

You may recall from an earlier chapter ("Being Crazy, Loving, and the Boiled Frog Syndrome") how people have a tendency to look for simple solutions, to deny the complexity of their experience, and to develop many problems from parent-child interactions. There were eight examples of "troubled" people who began as sensitive and aware children. The adults in their lives could not or chose to pay little attention to their feelings and sensitivity.

It bothers me that many adults believe their children are not absorbing what is going on around them. Parents tend to feel that their children lack the language skills to know what is going on. While it is true that **very** young children have no or few language skills, they do have physical and emotional responses to what happens around them.

It is fairly clear that an unborn child is affected to some degree by what her mother eats and drinks as well as her mood during pregnancy. It is even more clear that an infant's emotional relationship with the world can have long-standing effects. Very young children are processing what is going on in the family; from the very positive to the very negative. On the positive side, a child may be feeling tremendous warmth, caring, and connectedness with her family. On the negative side, she may be aware of loud screaming, fearfulness, demandingness, or looks that give her the impression she is "bad" or "ugly."

Your child's sensitivity is affected by what she absorbs, even if it's just at the feeling level. This sensitivity can be tricky; children often do not know what to do with it. It can get them involved in what is known as "magical thinking." For example, your child might begin to think that everything is her fault or problems are her punishment for something over which she has no control (helplessness). Of course, not everything is her fault nor are problems necessarily punishments. As you can imagine, magical thinking creates an additional burden on your child and may result in psychological problems. You may not be aware that this magical thinking is taking place.

Magical thinking may show itself in the way your child describes certain situations. From their strong sensitivity and potential for magical thinking, some children have been known to exaggerate or overly generalize. Many parents become quite upset when it appears that their children are lying or distorting the truth. Sometimes, they even fear a character defect in their children. Parents need to recognize that their children have limited experience, **which limits their sense of truth.** With this knowledge, parents might use their children's stories to detect the "magic" in their thinking and search for the underlying truth. This can be a difficult but worthwhile project.

I would like to offer an extremely interesting example of this. There was a child whose grandfather had died, and her mother discussed the concept of death with her. Later, her mother noticed that she was not eating and asked her about this. The child responded that if she did not eat, she would not grow up. If she did not grow up, then she could not die. This was her painful "interpretation" of this reality. Searching for the underlying truth was most helpful in this instance.

As a result, I would ask you to think about your child's exaggerations, generalizations, and creativity before you become judgmental and confrontative. If you consider the circumstances and the history of your child, you can distinguish between blatant lying and a child's lack of experience. Please remember, children do not have the experience or the capability to see things the way adults do.

Having concerns about your child's sensitivity and awareness does not imply that you should be overly protective or overly permissive. After extensive soul-searching, you may feel too much distortion is coming from your child. However, it is important that you not over-react to these distortions. You can enhance your sense of balance by remembering that this is another aspect of childhood experiencing and learning. If you provide solid, loving limits and empathetic discussions, these distortions will diminish over time, especially as your child integrates her experience with family reality.

Your adult reality is the task of accepting and affirming your child's sensitivity; therefore, helping her learn to balance creativity with the realities of her experience. "In balance" means not crushing her creativity. To provide this balance you will need to have an intense awareness of what is and what is not going on in the family. Your awareness of your child's sensitivity will allow you to pay attention to your child's process: to know that she is in a struggle, that she is aware of what is going on (at some level), and that she needs firm, loving guidance. She needs enough love in this guidance to balance out negative messages or possible magical thinking.

4. REMEMBER THAT CHILDREN ARE SMALLER IN SIZE.

Children, by virtue of being children, have a strong tendency to operate out of a physical sense of being. They are very aware of how much they are growing, who is stronger, who is the fastest, and so on. As smaller human beings, they are quite attuned to physical sensations, especially from adults. Physical sensations are magnified. As a result, loud voices often seem like screams to them. Yelling is often experienced as feeling struck (being hit). Verbal fighting between parents feels and seems like war. What seems like a slight pinch to an adult can be experienced as powerful pain to a child.

From the perspective of size, as well as the need for love, children can be humiliated quite easily. Virginia Satir, a well-known family therapist, has asked adults to participate in an exercise which allows them to experience this smallness. In this exercise, a standing adult leads or pulls around another adult who is on her knees. A physically inferior position literally changes the experiential world. With children's natural sensitivity, their smallness adds even more to the intensity of what they feel and perceive.

5. EVALUATE YOUR MARITAL RELATIONSHIP.

In light of your child's sensitivity, she is extremely aware (consciously and unconsciously) of what is occurring in your marriage. Thus, the quality of your marriage has the potential to profoundly affect your child and to leave a lasting impact on later years. While there are many, many books written about the positive and negative aspects of marriage, I would like to highlight some of the "destructive" tendencies that can occur. Please consider whether any of these tendencies occur in your marriage: controlling through physical violence, controlling through constant screaming, being overly critical, controlling with money, being physically or psychologically absent, fighting unfairly, punishing constructive emotionality, being overly manipulative, being disrespectful of others' needs, engaging in affairs, or being sexually demanding. These destructive tendencies create tension, which affects your child. Furthermore, your child may learn to be destructive as a result of this exposure.

If any of these tendencies exist in your marriage, I would ask you to consider and interpret the level at which they occur. Your consideration and interpretation may lead you to eliminate these destructive tendencies or to consider the possibility of a divorce. As you think about either alternative, I encourage you to seek either individual or marital therapy.

Thinking of divorce typically has two rather complex components. One component is concern for your own well-being. The second component is concern for your child; that is, the potential destructive effects if you stay married versus the potential destructive effects if you divorce. How you take care of yourself does provide a model of self-caring for your child. There is no doubt that children have a difficult time adapting to a divorce, and this is likely to carry over into their adult lives. Many individuals feel scarred by divorce. One major reason for this impact is that children have a need to preserve the unity of their parent's relationship. They know at a very deep level that it was this unity that brought them into the world. Accordingly, couples should make a good-faith effort to rid the relationship of any destructive tendencies through every means available to them. If both parents make a good faith effort, there is the strong possiblity that the marriage can become workable and serve as a positive model for their child.

However, there is also the possiblilty that one person will not cooperate in the good faith effort, or that **reality** will rear its ugly head. The reality is those serious personality differences that may exist between the couple. Although some personality differences do not seem to interfere with marriage, others create havoc within the relationship. Havoc typically destroys any outer sense of loving. As a result, the couple does not feel the loving beneath the differences and will lose this as a resource. Without this sense of loving, there is little motivation for marital change.

Personality differences can relate to interests in work, education, recreation, money, sex, and parenting. Personality differences can affect how two people relate emotionally and cognitively. One person might be very logical, and the other quite emotional. One person might be extremely neat, the other sloppy. These differences are magnified when two people lose their sense of love for one another.

If there is no interest in changing, or if the personality differences are too great, divorce becomes the only reasonable alternative to living in miserable unhappiness. Please notice that I am taking the position that you cannot make a "silk purse out of a sow's ear." While it is important to be positive about life, it is just as important to be honest about the reality of the relationship. If the possibility of a loving relationship is dead and you know that it is destructive to either you or your child, you must consider the possibility of divorce. Divorce may be the only sane thing to do. As one writer put it, divorce can be an honorable act. Otherwise, your child will learn and absorb these destructive qualities, or she will adapt destructively to a bad situation. Last, but not least, you serve as a negative role model by staying in a destructive relationship.

I do believe divorce is destructive, and I hope that you and your partner would make a "genuine good faith effort" to be loving in every way. Sometimes the threat of a divorce can open the eyes of a spouse so he or she will consider self-examination and growth. Of course, the decision is yours. I would that hope you would be very conscious and deliberate in your process. Admittedly, the decision to divorce is probably one of the most important decisions anyone can make. I wish couples would work harder in making the decision to be truly married or truly divorced. This decision has many implications for your child and other members of your family.

6. ENCOURAGE CHILDREN TO HAVE REALISTIC SELF-ESTEEM.

Human beings tend to see things in the extreme. These extremes may reflect your self-esteem; they can strongly affect your reactions, and your reactions affect your child. Extreme reactions are "black-white" reactions of good or bad, great or horrible; hot or cold; my child is flunking; my child is a genius; my child is going to be a juvenile delinquent, my child never does anything right, my child is a saint, my child is deliberately out to get me, and so on. These words suggest extremes in the same way that "black and white" suggest extremes. When words differ from reality, the effects are destructive.

Extremes also have a tendency to color our expectations, and as a result, change our reactions. For example, if I see my child as doing great in school, I am likely to expect "great" throughout. Then, if she happens to earn a "C," I am likely to overreact. The expectation of "great" influences my reactions. Many adults remember the intense focus of their parents on their "C" and the virtual ignoring of their "A"s and "B"s.

To help you further, I would like to discuss parents who feel their children "should" have the same values as they do. Frankly, it is quite easy to become distressed if you feel that your children have adopted a different set of values. The question is whether you will try to be constructive or allow your distress to carry you to extremes. While the nature of the value can differ from family to family, the concern is the manner in which the difference in value is handled. If the value of orderliness is violated, parents may have a tendency to refer to their child as a slob and shame her into compliance. If a child experiments with breaking the law of ownership, some parents may call their child a little thief. Of course, these parents have reason for concern, but their communication of extreme words is more destructive than helpful.

In their quest to be good parents, or simply in their natural behavior, parents often use such extremes as feedback to their children. This is unfortunate. Children who hear extremes begin to think in these terms and then begin to characterize themselves in these extremes, affecting their self-esteem. In this sense, they can easily come to think of themselves as good or bad, great or horrible, never able to do anything right, not good enough, or have a "why bother with anything" attitude.

I think it is much more realistic and useful to think in terms of factual observations, and from these observations, children can decide whether they like or dislike the behavior and its consequences. They will do this anyway. This judgment then comes from their own sense of factual observations and is not colored by excessive parental judgements. **Children's decisions about liking or disliking their behavior are very different from either liking or disliking themselves.**

On the opposite extreme, you may have the problem of giving your child praise that goes beyond her sense of reality. Her sense of reality is likely to be that she is learning, she is struggling, she makes "mistakes" that she regrets, and that she does not know how to handle all of her emotional energies. As a result, she is likely to be confused by receiving excessive and unwarranted praise. Sure, she is pleased with your being pleased but—she is going to begin to question how she can live up to your excessive praise and why your praise goes beyond her reality. It is then possible that she could create an internal expectation that she is unworthy, since the praise is unwarranted. Therefore, allow your praise and excitement to be in proportion to her struggle. Praise is certainly needed in proportional doses.

In this same vein, excessive or harsh criticism is very damaging. Unwarranted criticism creates negative expectations and negative self-esteem. A child who hears excessive criticism is prone to think that she is bad or incapable of doing things right. This instills a deep layer of fear and anger, which has the potential of occurring in the unconcious.

Instead of operating at extremes, please remember what I have already shared with you in the section concerning your child's process of development. Try to observe and focus on the process of what your child is trying to do, not on her personhood. Be positive without being extreme. Keep your enthusiasm in proportion to your child's reality. Do your best to get her to talk about what it is like for her to go through the process. Keep your own childhood issues in mind, so they do not negatively influence your reactions. Please remember that your major purpose is to instill self-confidence that is realistic, so that your child is neither overly hesitant nor overly confident.

7. BE ENCOURAGING.

Your child starts out physically small in a physically large world. At the same time, she is constantly facing a variety of new tasks that are quite challenging in one way or another. Last, but not least, small children exert a great deal of effort to please their parents. When you put these factors together, there is a great potential for excessive disappointment, humiliation, and feelings of failure as your child attempts to master new skills.

Most adults have forgotten what it was like to be a child living in a large world, pleasing parents, and dealing with daily challenges of one sort or another. If you can remember what it was like for you, you are much more likely to be encouraging as a way of helping her struggle.

Remember you are the adult and you have been through the struggle of development. By virtue of being a parent, you have designated yourself as your child's **guide**. With this in mind, you may provide balance by accentuating the positive without overdoing it. You may use the negative as an opportunity for learning. If you find yourself having a hard time with encouragement, please remove yourself for short periods of time while you think through your frustration. If you return with renewed energy and a realistic perspective, you will have found an excellent way of coping.

8. REMEMBER THAT CHILDREN WILL TEST LIMITS.

Parents frequently think and feel that their child will or should automatically do what is asked of her. If they realize she will not perform a task voluntarily, they then wish that she would automatically do it because they asked her to. I have had these thoughts and feelings myself. Life might be easier if this were the case, but then society would be producing robots, instead of developing people. These thoughts also apply to adults. It is incredibly amazing to me that so many adults do not do what is asked of them, even things that they themselves endorse. You might begin by considering your own reactions to requests, especially those which anger you. As human beings, we all have a side that is naturally egocentric. This reality requires patience and creativity.

Understanding that your child will not always be eager to do what you ask, that she might hesitate, and she may even say "no," will give you a more realistic parental perspective. While rebelliousness can be aggravating, you can expect a typical child to exhibit some misbehavior, even after correction. I am not preaching family anarchy, but a way of maintaining your perspective. Instead of expecting instant, perfect compliance, you may learn to expect less of the unwanted behavior. You will provide guidelines, guidance, and consequences. Children need this. The lack of limits and guidelines does not make children happy; instead it results in their being quite angry and confused. Neither do they need expectations of perfection. **Children need loving guidance which conveys caring about the relationship.**

Loving guidance requires balance in your emotional responses. Your responses should not suggest that she is "bad," or that she can have control by "pushing your buttons." If you react in such a way that your child thinks she has control over you, or if she actually does have control, you are in big trouble. If this is the case, it is time for you to do some deep soul-searching.

For example, if you are screaming over a trivial behavior, your child is now "in control" of your screaming and your feelings. Screaming over a trivial behavior is out of proportion to the behavior. Balance means understanding that you as the parent are encouraging a working relationship with a reduction in the frequency of the misbehavior. The best example is by utilizing words, feelings, and behavior that you want to teach. Your child must sense that you are teaching, and that a change in behavior will be beneficial to the relationship.

Without collaboration, a power struggle is likely to develop. Many parents do not collaborate for fear of losing the advantageous position of being the parent. Collaborating does not mean that you are your child's equal. It does mean giving your child the sense that she is important in the relationship, but not so important that she gains the upper hand. If you are successful, you can avoid an all-out war. It is now a fairly common belief that in an all-out war between parents and child, the child will win, usually at a great cost to her. Your task is to provide reasonable consequences and expectations, maintain the relationship, make an honest effort to collaborate in decision-making, and avoid an all-out war. You are much more likely to do this in a loving environment.

9. USE CONSTRUCTIVE INTERACTION AS A MEANS OF CONTROL.

If you will recall from Chapter 2, there is a constant interaction between internal experiences and external occurrences. As an example, think about going to bat and striking out. After a few strikeouts, you may become discouraged, saddened, angry, and find yourself not particularly motivated to keep trying. Your internal feeling is a function of the external experience.

You are the primary external experience in your child's life. It is of vital importance that **internal control** is learned from the interaction of internal feeling and external experience. Without internal control, your child will never have the resources to make wise decisions to benefit herself and others. She will be primarily motivated by external experience.

Learning of internal control will not occur if the interactions are destructive or vengeful. Destructive interactions are vindictive, excessively physical, and damaging to your child's self-esteem. Destructive interactions do not lead to learning about balanced sensitivity; they are likely to lead to intense power struggles. At best, the child's internal control will be overshadowed with fear, resentment, and possibly guilt.

Constructive interaction, on the other hand, allows your child to feel the connections between her behavior and the natural consequences of her behavior. Constructive interaction allows your child to see behavior change as beneficial to the relationship. Constructive interaction will demonstrate loving guidance and concern that is emotionally balanced. Your child may have hurt feelings in the interaction, but it will be with the knowledge that the pain can lead to learning. She will not perceive it as vindictive. This learning leads to balanced sensitivity.

If you have noticed, I have not yet defined constructive interactions; instead, I have described them. When I refer to constructive interaction, I mean an interaction that benefits both you and your child as you experience each other. This benefit may not be immediate, but it will be there. If you cannot see the movement toward benefit in your interactions, I would encourage you to give a great deal of consideration to these interactions. If these experiences are indeed constructive, you will eventually feel more positive with your child, and she with you.

"Constructive interaction" may become even clearer with the following example. Frequently, a parent with two children will observe that one of them is jealous of the time that the parent gives the other. Many parents will become quite frustrated and try to eliminate these feelings. The frustrated parent may even begin to favor the complaining child. Now think about how you might use constructive interaction as a means of dealing with sibling jealousy over time. Constructively, you might state your observations in a factual manner to the jealous child. In this vein, you might say, "You seem to be having difficulty with the way I treat you." Or you might ask for the jealous child's factual observations and feelings. You could ask for ways that this child would like "help" with her jealous feelings. You can work toward being respectful of the feelings while noting whether or not the jealousy is warranted. Then, as you spend time with each child, you can note that each of them deserves your full attention. You cannot do this if there is competition that interferes with your attention. As time progresses, using suitable words, you might ask the jealous child how she likes being the focus of attention. If you do not get hooked by any manipulations, you can constructively work your way through a difficult situation. Be positive. Be realistic, realize that some children are going to be resistant to constructive interaction. The more they are exposed to this type of interaction, the better your chances of succeeding with this strategy.

10. <u>AVOID HARSH WORDS</u>!

There is no way to have constructive interactions with harsh words. First, think of how these words feel when they are used on you. In my mind, harsh words are a form of emotional abuse. In fact, there has been a campaign by the National Committee for Prevention of Child Abuse pointing to "words that hurt." These words can range from very mild to severe. They all hurt, and each one has the potential to leave a lasting impression. They also leave a layer of resentment that creates a barrier to constructive interaction.

I would like to give you some ideas about the varieties of words that hurt. There are words that strike fear into a child's heart. For example, "If you don't take out the garbage, I will beat you until you can't see straight." A milder version is, "If you come home with a 'C', you can expect a spanking." Can you imagine what this child must think and feel when she goes to school every day? There are words that suggest that you do not love your child; words like, "I am going to send you away if you don't behave." Or words like, "I don't see how you can be a child of mine."

Then there are words that do not correspond to your child's reality. In essence, when you have not related to her reality, you leave your child to her own magical fantasies and do not provide affirmation for her internal struggle. While this is a milder form of harshness, it is still harsh. Imagine coming in from just being teased, and your parent says to you, "Don't worry about it; they don't know what they are talking about." You have just been told your pain does not count, and that you "should" think about something else. Harshness occurs when you are too busy to listen to your child, or when listening causes you obvious discomfort.

Last, but not least, is the abuse that occurs when you worry about what everybody else thinks. This is absorbed by your children. Again, think about this happening to you. For example, you come in from your job after being chewed out by your boss. Your spouse says to you, "You know your mother would really feel bad if she knew about this." How would you feel? The same is true if you are constantly telling your children to worry about what their grandmother, neighbor, or teacher is going to think. No one wants to constantly live in fear of what someone else is going to think or feel.

To avoid harsh words, you should listen to yourself and see how your words feel to you. (There is more on this in the communication chapter.) There is absolutely no place for name-calling. Words like "dummy," "stupid," and "worthless" are definitely emotional abuse. Consider your feelings and your actions with your child. Be positive; avoid the negative as much as possible. Remember how harsh words have affected you. When you find yourself being negative, take a "time-out" from your parenting. In other words, be conscious of your mood. If you are "unavailable," delay your discussion until you are available, caring and positive. This is also a way of taking care of yourself, while you eliminate the potential for destructive interaction.

11. DO NOT RESORT TO TACTICS OF GUILT TO BE IN CONTROL.

What is guilt? I am sure you have felt guilty, but you may not have thought about what guilt really is. There are words that are often used as substitutes for "guilt." These are "remorse," "shame," "blame," "fault," and "liability." These are powerful words, but they are not exact substitutes for guilt. There is also a psychological definition of guilt: anger turned inward. This internalization occurs rather frequently in our culture. If you begin to contrast the meanings of a word like "shame" and the meaning of "anger turned inward," you get two different experiences. If you contrast "remorse" with "anger turned inward," you get two different experiences. Which of these experiences would you like your child to have when she has done something "wrong"? I sure hope that your answer is remorse.

As you might now guess, the concept of guilt is filled with controversy. Many argue that we should feel guilty over what we have done that is "bad" or "wrong." Others argue that excessive guilt makes a child feel that she is "bad." The bottom line is whether your child feels badly about herself, or feels remorse over having performed some **major** misbehavior. I do not think it is in your child's best interest to incorporate "badness" into her self-esteem. If there is an underlying foundation of "badness," the potential to learn constructive interactions is diminished. Furthermore, badness cultivates further reasons for misbehavior. The child often thinks, "If I am this bad, I might as well as go ahead and be bad." If she is unhappy with her foundation, how can she be happy with any of the foundation's outgrowth.

I would like you to notice that I used the word "major" in front of misbehavior. What purpose would it serve to try to teach remorse for all infractions of the rules? Did you feel guilty when you were doing 65 in a 55 m.p.h. zone? There are people who wish you would feel guilty about speeding. Of course, this raises many philosophical questions that I cannot answer for you.

I do think it is useful and appropriate for your child to feel remorse over major misbehaviors that either hurt someone else or are hurtful to her. Teaching remorse is not always easy. Remorse begins by understanding that harm was done; the experience was either hurtful or of poor judgement. Instead of guilt, I propose teaching which emphasizes the reasons and outcomes of certain behaviors. By telling your child how something affects you along with how you feel (without blaming), you can provide an experience which demonstrates the values of what you want to teach. You might further encourage empathy by asking her how she would respond to similar circumstances. If needed, you can deliberately add consequences to the behavior. By providing a constructive experience concerning the effects of her behavior, you can then teach certain values.

Let me give you an example of teaching remorse or sorrow related to lying. First, I suggest considering whether a lying incident is part of a pattern or is rare. Next, I suggest you think about the purpose of the lie. Then, I would suggest sharing your thoughts and feelings about "receiving" a lie. It might sound like, "I am hurt that you gave me information that was not true, and I wonder what you had in mind in doing this." Or it might sound like, " I am very angry that you lied to me. What were you trying to achieve by changing the facts?" It could go on with a statement or question related to the effects of lying on a relationship. You might then ask how it would feel if her best friend lied to her about an important event. You could point out that the relationship could be damaged by the lack of trust. Finally, as you pick and choose your responses, you might suggest that you are very interested in being able to listen and to believe in her. These are important ingredients of a mutually collaborative relationship. By relating to her in this manner, you are modeling and suggesting an important value. It is called honesty.

It is entirely too easy just to give your child a value and expect her to follow it. Standing on "parenthood" as the reason for your values is not very constructive and is likely to fail. All this teaches is that you are the adult and she is the child—a version of might makes right. If the family lacks an atmosphere of caring, you may be left with an authoritarian relationship. Authoritarian relationships tend to teach shame and inward anger, which fuel the need for drugs and other acting-out behaviors. Guilt, in my mind, does not allow the ability or freedom to make wise choices.

On the other hand, remorse from experiential learning can make all the difference in the world. From loving, experiential learning, your child can experience the effects of her behavior. Experiencing consequences allows your child to learn values at a much deeper level and pass this gift on to others. Traditionally, guilt has not served this purpose in a useful manner.

12. AVOID PHYSICAL PUNISHMENT.

Physical punishment, as a general means of control, results in resentment, the lack of real respect, and teaches loss of control as an acceptable way of interacting. Spankings, beatings, and whippings leave a profound negative effect on both you and your child. However, in a rare instance, a spanking might be necessary as a **last resort** to get your child's attention. Notice, I am suggesting spanking only be used as a last resort and not in anger. This means your child is either in some imminent danger or that many repetitions of constructive interaction have failed. It is offered to emphasize a boundary, not "might makes right." Hopefully, your issues are not of power and control, but of having a collaborative relationship. As a quick aside, spankings are usually ineffective when your child has the unconscious or conscious sense of being in control.

13. DO NOT USE COMPARISONS AS A WAY OF OBTAINING CONTROL.

Comparisions to an older brother, younger sister, an uncle, or anyone else produce resentment. These comparisons can be quite obvious or they may be subtle. Children know that their sense of identity is violated by these comparisions. Violations of identity, as you well know, can have long-lasting effects. Your child wants and needs you to respond to her as an individual. Treating her as an individual allows you to be more in touch with the real relationship.

While not directly related to comparisions, treating a child as an individual raises another concern. There are parents who treat their child as part of a "collective." In other words, all of the children are the same. The children are not responded to as individuals, but as one of the children. Mary is not Mary; she's one of the children. In this instance, Mary could just as easily have a number and be responded to as child number two. Worse, some parents will punish all of the children for the wrong deeds of one of the children. Again, they are being treated as a collective. In this instance, the children are likely to experience the punishment as cruel and express resentfulness.

Children need to be recognized as individuals, and their individual qualities duly noted and appreciated. It is a violation of their identity to treat them as a reflection of a sibling. To punish a child for being a "reflection" further compounds the identity assault.

14. BALANCE THE NEEDS FOR DEPENDENCY AND BEING INDEPENDENT.

As is a great deal of parenting, this is a tricky tightwire for you to walk. Realistically, your children are dependent on you for both their physical and psychological needs. On the other hand, in the process of development, children are learning to do things on their own. I believe your child can best use her dependency as a springboard for being independent. If she knows you are there for support and guidance, she can then venture into new activities and discover her ability to master them. Knowing that you are there for support and guidance is essential. I call this her "childhood foundation." She knows that she is learning, and her learning is fraught with struggle. She needs a source of strength that is outside her own, which she can then incorporate into her own. Her dependency is not bad unless it is so intense there is no venturing into new activities.

Encourage your child to take reasonable risks and be there to support her if things do not go well. Use self-initiating phrases such as "It's your choice," "When you are ready," and "I'll let you decide." Or you might say, "If this does not work, we can decide what to try next." These phrases encourage your child's independence while allowing her to count on you for support. Relationships require a certain amount of dependency if they are to exist at all. **Needing someone in a realistic manner is a part of being human.**

15. LIVE IN THE MOMENT WITH YOUR CHILD.

It cannot be said often enough that the quality of your time is largely dependent upon your living in the moment. If you are not living in the moment, you and your child literally miss these moments. You can not relive them; they are history. In not living in the moment, you cannot experience the thoughts, the feelings and the spirituality of that moment. People miss the moment by either living in the past or in the future. It is easy to allow a past hurt or memory to interfere with the here and now. I have talked before about how your own childhood experiences can get in the way of looking at your child fully, personally. Seeing her fully is a part of the loving experience that makes life worthwhile. There is no way to see her if you are allowing the past and future to cloud your vision.

Of course, to really live in the moment, you must recognize that you have a past that precedes each moment and a future that follows it. By understanding the impact of your past, you can work with it so that it does not get in the way of the present.

The future provides its own form of interference. For example, many adults are afraid to play sports because they might fail (a judgment measured by a future standard). Failure is then a function of the future; it takes you from the present. You are doing something for an external reason, winning. Winning occurs at the end of a match or game, not in the moments of playing. If you play to win, you are going to have trouble concentrating on the moment. Lack of concentration interferes with playing. If you want to concentrate on playing, you must practice to play in the moment, and then you will tend to play better. If you play better, your chances of winning are improved. Consequently, winning is not the ultimate goal. With this attitude, you combine the future with focusing on the here and now.

I have found that the processing of experiences as they happen is often more meaningful than the end result. Winning is not "everything." Instead, my experiences leave a lasting impression, which, in turn, affects many "end results." While these end results are and have been very important to me, I wish I had concentrated more on the experiences. If I had, my life experiences would have been dramatically different and more complete.

If you concentrate as much on the moment as on the end result, your life is going to be more balanced. Foolishness or impulsiveness through ignoring the past or future is unwise. With past experiences as a foundation and with concentration on the present moment, you will enhance the meaning of the future.

16. PROVIDE A GOOD MODEL FOR EATING AND PHYSICAL EXERCISE.

It is very clear that your child's physical and mental health run hand-in-hand. If your child is full of unhealthy substances, she will function less well. The same is true of being overweight or in poor physical health. You do not need to become a food or an exercise fanatic to be a good model. In fact, being a fanatic may teach negative self-esteem. I encourage you to show a healthy respect for your physical self as well as for the physical condition of your child. I also encourage further relationship enhancement through joint physical activities.

17. BE A MODEL OF A PERSON WHO IS EMOTIONALLY BALANCED.

I could say a lot here about being emotionally balanced. However, there is a chapter devoted to emotionality. For now, I would like to say that emotional balance means keeping your feelings in perspective and expressing your feelings without being destructive. Balance requires understanding overly intense emotions to situations. When you are in balance, you are supportive of others' emotions, but are not manipulated by their feelings. Balance requires that your feelings be used as an expression of an internal state and not to control others. Feelings are an internal feedback mechanism to let you know what is going on inside yourself. Expressing and acknowledging your feelings can have very positive effects on your insides; however, they may not change your external reality. Expressing and acknowledging your feelings will change your experience.

18. BE A MODEL OF A PERSON WHO FEELS CONFIDENT AND SECURE.

The reasons for this are fairly obvious. Your confidence in your abilities and your acceptance of your deficiencies allows your child to see you as an adult able to deal with reality. This affects how you interact with your entire family. This also teaches your child these same qualities! There is an old saying that "a little knowledge is dangerous." This is true. It is very important to know your limits. You give your child permission to acknowledge her limits by openly acknowledging what you don't know. **Confidence and security is knowing what you don't know!**

I have emphasized your limits in the above paragraph so that you will struggle with what you know and what you don't know. This struggle will help you clearly define what you do know, what you feel, and where you need to continue to search. This process will enhance your ability to act on your knowledge. You can feel good about the growth you have achieved and can use your limits as your growing edge for further struggle. Feeling confident and secure is knowing your parenting is a struggle, and you will use the struggle wisely.

19. DO NOT ATTEMPT TO BE A "GOOD" OR "PERFECT" PARENT.

The "good" or "perfect" parent operates out of what she thinks "should be" rather than what is. This is dangerous. What should be is not necessarily what really is. For example, how many people have you met who were always happy parents? Some of these people may have felt that they "should" be happy. Having a "should" does not make it so! To be good or perfect implies a formula for doing the "right" thing. Unfortunately, (or maybe fortunately) each child-family combination is different, so reality requires a close examination of what is actually happening in the family. This means that finding the right thing to do is not always easy. Instead, I would suggest that you look at who your child is and what kind of history she has had. What is her temperment? How have certain influences affected her? How has she fared in her quest to be a person?

20. GET DOWN TO YOUR CHILD'S LEVEL AND PLAY.

It is extremely important for a child to know that her parents can come down to her level and have fun. There are at least three reasons for this. The first is that having fun together offers another dimension of intimacy. The second is that it provides a balancing experience to seriousness in the family. Third, your having fun provides permission for the family to have fun. Fun allows spontaneity, and spontaneity enhances living in the moment. This is truly a richer way to live.

21. LET YOUR CHILD SPEAK OPENLY.

Speaking openly is quite the opposite of the way things were in the old days, the days when a child was to be seen and not heard. There are a couple of good reasons for letting your child speak openly. First, children are prone to keep their deepest thoughts to themselves, and these thoughts can easily turn into "magical" thinking. Second, by encouraging openness, you enhance the possiblities of good communication. In allowing your child to speak openly, you are letting her know that you are interested in what she has to say and think. This does not mean being permissive. This does not include name-calling or calling someone's character into question, or letting your child push you around with words.

Some parents are overly concerned about their children being disrespectful or "talking back;" others just want to keep their children quiet. "Disrespectful" and "talking back" can mean anything you want them to mean. Do not use these words to squash your child's talking and thinking. You might squash her talking but **you cannot control her thinking.** The end result is resentment. You can use the words "disrespectful" and "talking back" to describe those concepts when your child has truly crossed over the line into destructive interaction.

Take time to encourage your child to talk about her thoughts and feelings. This allows you access that you otherwise would not have. Be open to your own thoughts and feelings. This will help your child understand that it is OK to talk about personal matters. Personal communication is essential for an intimate personal relationship.

22. BE RESPONSIBLE FOR YOURSELF.

If you make yourself **totally** responsible for your child, how will she learn to be responsible for herself? Excessive responsibility teaches confusion between her sense of identity and yours. Because the sense of identity is very important to emotional well-being, this confusion often leads to emotional difficulties. Hopefully, over time, you are slowly and progressively teaching your child to be a separate individual from you.

Being responsible means knowing what you have done and what your child has done. Being responsible means "owning" your own thoughts, feelings, and behaviors and not blaming someone else. Many authors have suggested that the way to understand responsibility is to break the word into two words—"response" and "able." This means you are able to make and choose your own responses. It means you understand there are influences on behavior, and you choose to give power to one influence over another. If the idea of influence and power is confusing, please return to the chapter entitled "What Makes People Tick."

There are many ways to be irresponsible. One major way is to feel that you are unable to make a response to situations that need a response. Not deciding (over time) is deciding to keep things the way they are. Obviously, this is not a good example for your child. Another form of irresponsibility is to feel and communicate that your child is making you "mad," "crazy," or "driving you to leave home." At times, you may feel this way. However, assigning responsibility to your child for your feelings gives away your power and makes life even more difficult. Remember, there is your personal power, and then there is the power you give to others. This happens frequently when parents use their child to make up for something missing "out of" their childhood. I hope you will be very conscious of this common tendency.

Please be careful of your example when you communicate power and influence in your marriage. This can be either a good or bad example to your child. You are responsible for what you do, and your child is learning she is responsible for what she does: response-able. As a parent, your responsibility for care includes the obligation to provide your child with the best influence you can. Please do not forget that ultimately your responsibility stops at the edge of your skin, and that your child's responsibility begins at the edge of her skin.

You can find all kinds of ways to influence, but ultimately she will make her own choices. While this often scares parents, it is a fact; your child will make her own choices. As she chooses, she will learn how her internal processing goes with each choice. She will also learn how her choices result in mutual experiences with you and with others. She can learn dependency within the limits of response-ability.

23. EVALUATE EXPERIENCES WITH YOUR CHILD.

While there are too many experiences for you to examine each one, it would be helpful for you to spend a few minutes each night thinking about the day's events. Note the negative experiences and how they did not go well. Think about how you and your child could have been different with one another. Notice that this involves an understanding of everyone's contributions without blaming. Try to fantasize how your child was thinking and feeling in these situations. See if you can't use this information to influence future interactions. Balanced evaluations keep you from repeating the same pattern over and over. Noting the positive experiences will help you remember and enhance future interactions.

If you begin early in your parenting, there could be a place for family evaluations. Some individuals will object to family evaluations for the sake of time or the age of the children. If so, you might want to consider the time and energy "wasted" when there is little if any collaboration.

24. USE FAMILY MEETINGS FOR EVALUATION AND COMMUNICATION.

There will certainly be family conflicts, and one way to resolve them is through communication and teaching at the time of the conflict. As conflicts occur, tension may grow, and you may need to clear the air. By this, I mean a time in which all family members have a chance to speak both their feelings and their sense of solution to ongoing difficulties. Family meetings can be used as a vehicle for airing problems and struggling with mutual goals; this gives a sense of family input into the rules. Hopefully, everyone's feelings, thoughts, and spirit are considered.

The family meeting can be obstructed by any one person

deciding that her needs are the only needs that count. For the family meeting to work, mutual cooperation is essential. This can be enhanced if you act as an effective moderator by encouraging honesty about past behavior, staying with the point of the discussion, minimizing angry outbursts, and being open to different possibilities for a solution. This does not mean giving up your right to a final say-so. Thus, the process is a delicate one; your attempts to be open, honest, and fair must be evident.

25. <u>PUTTING IT ALL TOGETHER</u>.

I am not sure how you might feel after reading these 24 points of establishing a good relationship. Every person is different. I do know that it would be hard for me to remember all of these as I go through my daily life. I do think there are some highlights that will be beneficial throughout your child's journey. I would encourage you to be very loving and considerate. Feel your own feelings and be in tune with the feelings of others. Listen to yourself and listen to others. This calls for a real sense of balance. Question yourself when things do not feel good. Use this questioning to understand your own thoughts and feelings. Pay attention if you lack a sense of feeling alive. If you are tense, learn to relax. When it is time, laugh and have fun. "Live your life with heart."

I would like to close this chapter with a quote from Stephen Howard, M.D., which appeared in an issue of *Pilgrimage*[1]

> "Success in intimate relationships requires equality of power, openness and honesty, a willingness to be responsible for oneself in one's entirety, and a desire to accept and appreciate our differences."

While it is impossible to have equality of power in a parent-child relationship, parents can work at giving their children enough power to learn that they are competent, loveable, and able to work at being open with their innermost selves. From this power, they, too, can accept positive differences in a loving way.

Chapter 5

COMMUNICATION

"Communication is the heart of love, the sacred vessel from which we pour the wine of our souls."[1]

John O. Stevens[2] has written powerfully, "My living becomes split between image and reality, between what I think I am and what I am." You may want to read this again. These words describe how we live and how we communicate our living. As they describe the way we live, they are integral to the process of communication. I hope you find these words powerful.

This quote suggests people are not always what we perceive them to be, nor are they always what they perceive themselves to be. Please consider this two-part process. First, there is communication **about** people which is not always accurate. This communication is from others **about** others. Consequently, a child struggles with the differences between information given and her own perceptions of the way people really are. Children are very accurate (sometimes brutally so) in most of their perceptions . For example, Aunt Minnie may be described as a very nice lady, but your child notices she often gives very short, angry, sarcastic responses. Being labelled nice while being angry and sarcastic is difficult for a child to compute.

Second, there is communication from people which is not always accurate about who or what they really are. This is communication from persons about the portrayal of themselves. In reality, we often deny, minimize, exaggerate, and distort our self descriptions. You can probably recall many instances of disagreement

113

with someone else's self-description. With this in mind, you might want to revise your own self-description.

What is it like for a child to be in this world of communication? What is it like for your child? Remember, children are in the process of development; they are sensitive, perceptive and very emotionally aware. They know when words do not match truth and reality. Authentic communication requires truth and reality; truth and reality require authentic communication. Truth, reality, and authenticity are the oppositites of craziness. When people are not what they seem, either to themselves or to others, is it any wonder things do not make sense, that there is anger, a denial of reality, and the world is portrayed as a storybook fantasy? Accurate communication of truth and reality is essential.

Communication is the imparting of a message or information from one person to another. Communication is also the imparting of information within the basic parts of a person. We all talk to ourselves through thinking. If communication is inaccurate, there is the potential for many problems. This now brings me to the major point of my communication overview: if you are not communicating from an accurate sense of your inner self, you cannot accurately communicate your inner sense. You can not have an accurate inner sense if there is a difference between reality and your image of reality. Without an accurate inner sense, you impart inaccurate information to yourself and others, including your child.

At some level, most people know if their image of reality is different from reality. On the other hand, many do not want to know the extent of the difference between their image and reality. With this split, a person will lack the confidence of someone who has a firm grasp of what they feel, what they think, and what they believe. Feelings, thoughts, beliefs, and behaviors need to work together smoothly to impart a sense of personal power. This is referred to as confidence and self-esteem.

With personal power, the world can make more sense, there is no need for the denial of reality, and the world is portrayed (pretty much) as it really is. With personal power, you can communicate accurately with yourself and others. The ability to communicate fully

114

and accurately is a clear sign that you have access to your inner self. It is also a clear sign that your basic parts work well together. When your thoughts, beliefs, feelings and actions are aligned, you function at a higher level, which allows you to communicate at a much higher level. With a higher level of accurate communication within ourselves and between ourselves, we can live more fully and reduce the amount of craziness within our culture.

1. BE ASSERTIVE WITH YOUR WORDS.

To be assertive means to say clearly what you think and feel. To be assertive means that you are willing to take care of yourself, you recognize your needs, and are willing to balance them with the needs of others. It also means you are sensitive to the effects of your words. This does not imply that your words will never be hurtful, because telling the truth can be hurtful. Being assertive needs to come from a "centered" place so that you are capable of using words to express feelings in a constructive way. This prevents a backlog of unresolved feelings from getting in the way of your being balanced.

Being assertive is also a sign that you feel good enough about yourself to care about the meaning and the delivery of your communication. You feel sure of the intent of your communication. This means that you trust your inner sense of balance and care enough to "stick to your guns." If you lose your sense of balance and allow your negative side too much power, you could easily move into aggressive or passive communication.

Aggressive communication is destructive in many ways. The National Committee for Prevention of Child Abuse wisely noted in its advertising, "Words hit as hard as a fist." Yet it is so easy, if you do not pay attention, to become aggressive when your child does not do what you want. We think children are simply supposed to do what their parents tell them to do, without any negative feelings. It is as if children are only an extension of their parents.

Many parents **seem** to believe that aggressive communication will encourage a child to be a "better" child. They act as if they believe put-downs and pushiness will manipulate their child into behaving. While this might work to achieve a short-term goal, it ignores the process and the negative long-term effects on a child. Aggressive communication only encourages a child to feel badly about herself. Disrespect breeds disrespect.

Here are some examples of aggressive communication which are pushy and abusive: "stupid; lazy; when are you going to straighten up?; if you loved me, you would . . . ; you make me mad; you disgust me; you are going to be a bum; you never do what you are told; you are bad; you're going to Hell (you may be a parent, but you are not God); you ought to be ashamed; you are driving me out of the house; how could you do this to me?; why aren't you grateful?; when are you going to act your age?; don't be a baby; grow up; you are just like your father; you are just like your mother; you never listen; who do you think you are?; your brother never did this sort of thing;" and on and on, and on. How do these phrases feel when you imagine hearing them? Imagine a child hearing them. It is tragic that these abusive phrases are so widely used.

Lastly, aggressive communication is confusing; it does not provide direct, respectful communication about what behavior is wanted or requested. Instead, it violates and attacks another person's identity.

If you or another person in the family is prone to use these phrases, please do whatever you can to stop this abusive language. You may refer to the "harsh words" section in the guidelines of Chapter 3. If necessary, get professional help.

I have "talked" to you about assertive and aggressive communication. There is a third type—passive communication. Passive communication does not clearly say what you want to say; it is indirect. Passive is saying you want your child to respect your wishes about time when you really want her to be in by six o'clock. Passive is telling your spouse you would like her to be home more, when you really want more one-to-one attention. Passive communication results from fearfulness of what may happen if you direct messages to particular difficulties or problems. People who do not speak their minds and feelings tend to have unresolved feelings of fear and resentment.

Some people refer to this as a "yucky" feeling, and others refer to it as feeling "their tail is between their legs." Either way, these individuals know they have succumbed to inhibition and have not given their true thoughts and feelings a voice. In addition, others have not been allowed to know the individual's true wants and desires. The ability to give your thoughts and feelings a voice is a powerful measure of your self-esteem. Knowing and expressing your distinctive voice is essential to overcoming inhibitions and recovering wholeness.

As you can tell, there are great differences between aggressive, passive, and assertive communication. The first two express a lack of respect for others as well as self. Aggressive communication attacks your child's self-esteem instead of providing a clear message of what you really want. In fact, the violation of self-esteem prevents a child from hearing other parental messages. Passive communication also leaves your child with no clear idea of what is wanted. This forces her into "mind reading" and sets her up to be wrong, to feel helpless, inadequate, and insecure. Assertive communication tells her exactly what you want, and she can feel secure in the clarity of the message. It also serves as a model for her to communicate with others. Last, but not least, she can be included in the process of assertive communication so that she feels a part of the family process. Assertiveness is a benchmark for respectful communication and good self-esteem. How you and your spouse communicate will be the model for your child.

> **"Artful communication connects us to each other; bonds us together through strands of energy, actions and words. We need to ask ourselves if these strands are made up of kind and gentle pearls or prickly thoughtless barbs?"**[3]

2. AVOID OBSTRUCTIVE MESSAGES.

Obstructive communication is similar to aggressive communication in that it stops the interaction cold in its tracks. While obstructive communication does not attack another person's character, it clearly tells the other person you are not interested in communicating. You obstruct the communication process. Let me provide you with some common examples: "I don't want to talk about it; just forget it; leave me alone; if that's what you think;" and the cruncher, "I'm leaving." There may be times when you are too emotional or unclear to talk; it would be better to clearly say you need some time and do not want to stop the communication. If you are able to offer reasons, it would be helpful. Asking for time is obstructive only if you do not intend to return to the conversation. Awareness of obstructive messages in your family can help you reply with consciousness.

3. <u>MUCH IS COMMUNICATED WITHOUT WORDS</u>.

A smile, a frown, a twisted face, or a glancing look can communicate a powerful message to your child. There is no such thing as silence between two people. There is only the absence of words. A story of a woman who could not speak her mind to a salesperson offers an example of this power. When asked why, she said it was because of the way he looked at her. It turned out she had very painful memories of adults looking at her. The similarities in facial and eye expression reminded her of these painful memories. In another instance, a man said his father never had to punish him; his father would just look at him and he would turn into a "puddle of water." Much is communicated without words. Often, parents are unaware of their facial expressions and the messages they convey.

In addition, there are other "silent" forms of communication. In most instances, these messages convey more power than words alone. For example, touching and hugging typically express great levels of loving. Experiencing someone actually crying (with tears) is very different from having someone say that they are sad. Observing someone's eyes can often tell you more than their words. There is great truth in the saying "the eyes are the windows to the soul."

Although words are obviously important to communication,

there are many times where they just cannot convey the internal experience. I wish I had a nickel for every instance when I did not have the words to reflect my feelings. Words can be extremely powerful; they can be very cutting or very loving. If you will think about your own life, **you will realize the power of how and what you communicate.** As you realize this, you will also realize the power of what your child receives.

4. USE "I", "YOU", AND "WE" ACCURATELY.

These pronouns can be quite confusing when they are used interchangeably. As I communicate something of myself, the appropriate pronoun is "I." Unfortunately, many people use a generic "you" when referring to themselves. For example, I might say "you go the store" when in actuality I mean "I go to the store." When "I" want something, it is not "you" wanting something. The concise use of "you" refers to another person, not yourself. I hope you are getting the sense of how confusing this can be.

"You" reflects your sense that the other person is separate from you. While this may seem like a trivial issue at first, if you think about it, the importance becomes obvious. Your child is learning to be psychologically separate from you. Although these words are not the most important factor in her separating, they can reduce the confusion in the separation process. Hence, using the correct "I" and "you" can help her sense of separateness. This is also helpful for communication of "I" messages and feelings. The pronoun "we" is only to be used when people are actually doing something together.

5. WHEN IN DOUBT, CLARIFY FOR YOURSELF.

Communication tends to be a very confusing process in this society. Either people do not know how to say what they really mean, or they are inhibited in saying what they really mean. And, of course, there is the third possibility—some people deliberately lie. It appears there is a tendency to be sociable, nice, and political on the one hand, and aggressive on the other.

When you feel it is important, do not hesitate to clarify an unclear or confusing message. You might consider using one of the following methods: 1. repeat what you thought you heard; 2. ask for the message in different words; or 3. ask a question that would clarify the communication. It is better to find ways to check out what you have heard than to **assume** you know. Also, asking for clarification can be a fascinating process. You may find that what you "heard" was not the intended message. This also allows the speaker to think about her chosen words. With the process of checking it out, you are much more likely to learn the intended message. You then have obtained clarification.

6. GET TO THE POINT.

Much of what is important can be said in very few words. Adding unnecessary words can confuse your message. There are people who will use the extra words to either twist your message or to manipulate you in their interest. You are likely to feel uncomfortable when this happens. Please pay attention to your discomfort, as this can be a signal that you are not being heard. Children can be especially adept at finding ways to use your words against you. Keep in mind the thoughts from Chapter 3 that children will naturally test limits, especially when they have had previous success in doing this. Make your point and be heard; do not permit yourself to be manipulated. Emphasizing your point with conciseness streamlines communication.

7. AVOID "SHOULD'S" AND "OUGHT TO'S".

I suspect that the notion of avoiding "should's" and "ought's" could be controversial. "Should's," "should not's," "ought's," and "ought not's" are common in our language, and they appear to be essential in demanding behavior changes in children. How else are we going to tell our children what we want and what we expect? If you have noticed, even I have sprinkled a few "should's" throughout this writing. It may be impossible to completely eliminate "should's" and "ought's," but there are three important reasons for being careful about their use: 1. "should" and "ought" do not reflect what is; 2. these words represent a higher authority than you as a parent; someone else's ideal; 3. self-esteem can be negatively affected by them. The following provides more detail to these reasons.

The first reason is that "should" and "ought" do not make any real sense. Life is really not made up of "should's" and "should not's." Life is what it is. If you say something should have happened, you mean it did not happen. If something should not have happened, this means it did happen. While this may not confuse you, think what it must be like for a three or four-year-old. Listen as a young child as I repeat this for you: "If something should have happened, it did not happen. If something should not have happened, it did happen." Can you sense the confusion in trying to know what happened and what was supposed to happen?

Remember, you are a small child and do not understand fully what is going on. I strongly believe that people are confused between what is, and what should be. In order to give a straight message, tell your child exactly what you, want rather than using "should's and "should not's." Your child is much more likely to understand a request for something specific than talking about something that did not happen. If it had happened, you would not be using these phrases. This is a very experiential kind of thing.

The second reason is much easier to understand. Again, think of this from the perspective of a young, developing child. The second reason is these words represent a higher authority than you as a parent. I firmly believe in higher authority, and it makes sense that children come to understand this concept. However, at a young age, children first recognize higher authority through interaction with their parents. If I say, "You should not steal," I am implying that a higher authority than myself feels strongly about stealing. A young child cannot perceive who this higher authority is. Children take in the behavior, thinking, feelings, and spirituality of their parents and then use what is absorbed to connect to the outside world. This is the learning of higher, universal authority. Thus, it is essential to lay down a foundation of humans relating to humans in a loving relationship.

Constructive communication is concerned with the benefits to the relationship, as well as to specific values. Thus, if I am trying to teach my child not to steal, I would first emphasize the impact on our relationship, as well as the impact on any other relationships. The experience is personalized when I tell her I do not want her to steal, why I feel this way, and there will be consequences if she steals. By doing this, I am exercising, as well as emphasizing, my own sense of personal, internal power instead of parental power. This interchange communicates my personal values. Because my child and I are relating at a personal level, there is an increase in the intensity of her experience with me.

I strongly advocate much more powerful, loving interactions with your child; this will greatly enhance her experience and relationship with you. As your child matures, this personalized relationship can then connect her more fully with the outside world. Positive, personal family relationships enable connections to "higher authority." I am not saying a child cannot connect without a positive, personalized family relationship, but it is a powerful factor in enhancing higher authority connections. "Should's" and "should not's" do not provide this experience by themselves, they are too impersonal. It is essential she experience the effects of behavior on relationships. Higher authority has no meaning unless she connects through immediate experience.

As an example, consider a mother who tells her child what to do in order to avoid her father's punishment. Now put yourself in the child's shoes. Are you learning about your relationship with your mother, or are you learning fear of what your father might do? If you are just learning fear, what are you learning about relationships? What are you learning about higher authority? To tell your child that she is going to face her father sabotages your power as well as the relationship she might have with him. If she has a poor relationship with you and is afraid of her father, what is the likelihood that she is going to connect with the positive values of the world?

In other words, I strongly believe the foundation of higher authority starts with the foundation of good family relationships involving positive values. Without good relationships, the values

122

are in danger. "Should's" and "should not's" cannot carry the burden of parenting: they do not add to a sense of personal relationship. They do add a sense of power (however falsely) to hierarchical relationships.

There is a third reason for limiting the use of "should's" and "ought-to's." Again, please try to think of this from the standpoint of a developing three- or four-year-old child. In fact, let's pretend you are a three-year-old in the grocery story playing with a package of gum that is about to open. Your parent says to you, "You should not play with that, it is about to open, and it has not been paid for." What do you feel? Now pretend the parent is fairly angry with you and again says, "You should not play with that!" What do you feel? Now pretend the parent is very angry and screams, "YOU SHOULD NOT PLAY WITH THAT!!" What do you feel? What kind of mental image are you likely to form from this experience?

When a child hears these kinds of "shoulds," she is likely to question her own character. The conscious or unconscious question goes like this, "**What is wrong with me that I could do such a thing?**" While this is not likely to happen at the conscious level, the "should" sends a negative reflection of her character. At the unconscious level, she may "record" this as badness, inadequacy, or pure helplessness. As another example, hear the character implication in the following, "You should have brought home better grades." While this may be true, your child's self-esteem will not be helped or improved by these words.

I have deliberately gone into detail about the subtle and not so subtle effects of "should" and "should not." What I have said is equally true for "ought" and "ought not." Clearly, as a parent, you want to teach loving, assertive ways of being. This is your role. Please think about how you are accomplishing this.

If you want to change your child's behavior, try to understand the circumstances and the internal motivation of a particular behavior. How would you want to be taught this change of behavior? You can then decide what action you need to take to encourage this change in behavior. You can even make requests without using "should." Using the gum example, you could say, "Please leave the gum on the shelf as it is about to open and I will be upset." More importantly, you can develop positive statements about the effects of behavior on relationships and values. You then build her character, rather than tearing it down. You might also incorporate the ideas of the "Discipline" chapter in your request for a change in behavior. There is no reason for you to be an unassertive parent. As you grow in your knowledge of loving behavior within the context of boundaries, you will find many ways to assert a balance between the needs of your child and the world that surrounds her.

8. MAKE REQUESTS OF YOUR CHILDREN.

We all like to be asked to do something rather than to be ordered. Children are no exception. However, children do need to learn that requests are often polite ways of being told what to do. This is the way of much of the world. Requests may also be used effectively to ask for a change in behavior, but be prepared to become more forceful, especially when it is important and your requests are not being heard. If you do need to be more forceful, you can accomplish this in a positive way. Instead of asking, "Would you please pick up your socks?", you might say, "Please pick up your socks." You might also respect your child's ability as a problem-solver by simply saying, "Your socks are on the floor." Your parental responses require balanced sensitivity to you and your child's needs.

9. AVOID COMMUNICATION POWER STUGGLES.

Fighting seems to be a part of human nature. However, fighting can be constructive, or it can be destructive. Constructive verbal fighting can lead to enhanced feelings of intimacy. Destructive fighting leads to disaster. Physical fighting is nothing more than determining who has the most physical power. It is always destructive and has no place in intimate relationships.

Verbal fighting can be similar if the purpose of the fight is simply to win. This is a power struggle. Power struggles absolutely undermine mutual communication. I would now like to give you a wonderful observation from Dr. Wayne Dyer. He has stated, "Virtually all fights revolve around the absurd thought, if only you were more like me, then I wouldn't have to be upset."[4] I hope that it reminds you of Stephen Howard's words in the "Putting It All Together" section of Chapter 3. Dyer also aptly notes that "People are not going to be different simply because you would like it to be that way."

You are in deep trouble if you think your child is going to think and behave exactly as you do. You are in deep trouble if you think your child will act in the proper way simply because you say it is proper. Unless you and your child operate from a mutual communication point of view, you are going to have an intense power struggle on your hands. A power struggle means it is your power versus hers. If this is happening on a frequent basis, you have a significant problem. If you and your child engage in a power struggle, she is going to win. This may possibly be at her own expense, but she certainly has the power to win. This reminds me of an old saying, "When one person loses in a relationship, the relationship loses."

To nurture your relationship, it is very important to encourage mutual communication. You can do this by saying "How can we work this out so we both feel OK?" This does not mean capitulating to your child. It does mean fully considering your motives and your expectations, along with your child's. This approach teaches your child, by your example, to think about other people and to balance her needs with the needs of others. Otherwise, you have extremes. For those of you who might be panicked at the idea of mutual communication, I assure you that your child will learn to discriminate between those times in which a mutual solution is possible and those times in which your limits are very clear and firm.

There will be fights and even some power struggles. The trick is to resolve them in mutually satisfying ways over time. Here are several suggestions to minimize their occurrence: The first is to be interested in a mutual relationship and to make this evident in your thoughts, feelings, behavior, and spirit. Your child can and will detect any "cracks" in your intentions. If you find yourself in a power struggle, please question the reasons for its occurrence. Ask yourself if you are determined to have your child be just like you or to what degree she can be different from you. This requires honesty and consciousness.

As you talk with her, acknowledge her thoughts and feelings. Let her know your own thoughts and feelings, especially about how the fight affects relationships. Do not allow the conversation to sway from the fight unless it is clear the fight is about something else. Be clear about picking a time for the fight that is conducive for resolving the fight. Do not allow name-calling or character assassination. Do not focus on your child's weak spots in order to win the fight. Use "I" statements with regard to your thoughts, feelings, and opinions. Do not threaten your child with physical punishments; threats may temporarily end the fight, but it will not resolve the issue (Adults can practice this with one another as well). Threats may cause her to go underground. Focus on the behavior you would like from her, not on what she is doing wrong. Be sensitive to the anger (yours and hers), and as the two of you calm down, try to have some sort of summary to signify the importance (or lack of it) of the fight. The content of the summary is geared to the maturity of your child.

Please remember that mutual communication does not mean giving your child excessive power. If you can both remember the highest good is mutuality, you will both struggle to maintain the relationship. In the process, you will both learn that mutual relationships can tolerate and support struggle. In fact, if there is real mutuality, your relationship will be strengthened by the struggle. This comes from an expansion of boundaries through caring and knowing you are there for one another. Through this process, she learns collaboration with others within a mutually caring relationship.

"If our intention is to win or to be right, we'd better pause until we can change that to a desire for better understanding and more connection. Needing to win and be right doesn't come from our hearts and souls and only evokes shame and defensiveness in others."[5]

---

10. AVOID DISTORTIONS IN COMMUNICATION.

Virginia Satir[6] has outlined several ways communication may be distorted. One way is to placate. To placate, you will agree, say "yes," or use false words in order to avoid upsetting the other person. A second way is to find fault or blame in reaction to a message. Many people have a tendency to feel criticized when an observation is made, and then attack. This is in lieu of just being open to the meaning of the message. A third way to distort communication is to talk like a computer, so that everything is ultra-reasonable, calm, and logical. Life is certainly not like this. Parents sometimes use this technique to suppress the emotionality of the family. The fourth way is to be a distracter. This simply means that you move away from the central point of discussion. This can be subtle or very obvious. Subtle distractions are often referred to as "taking tangents, sidetracking, or sidestepping the issue." No matter what you call it, the distraction attempts to take people away from the major focal point. Any distortions in communication will add to the difficulty of communicating and will add to the possiblity of destructive family relationships. Some distortions create craziness, either in this book's sense or in a psychiatric sense.

11. EVALUATE YOUR MAJOR COMMUNICATION ROADBLOCKS.

Experiences with myself and others suggest that most communication roadblocks stem from a variety of fears. These include: 1. I might make a mistake; 2. I might say the wrong thing; 3. someone might not like me; 4. I might hurt someone's feelings; 5. someone might find out who I really am; 6. I might not be perfect; 7. someone might reject me; 8. I fear that another person might not be able to say "no" to me; 9. everything I say must be loving; 10. I am just afraid. There are self-esteem problems when people have something to say, but are afraid to say what they think and feel. Often, if their fears are repeated out loud or written, the intensity of these fears will lessen. This is another form of increased consciousness.

12. BE AN ACTIVE LISTENER.

> "Deep listening is miraculous for both listener and speaker. When someone receives us with openhearted, non-judging, intensely interested listening, our spirits expand.[7]

Listening is an active process as opposed to a passive one. You must be truly interested and willing to hear what your child is saying. In this active process, your child will feel you are responsive to her thoughts and concerns. Again, this does not mean being manipulated if her thoughts and concerns are destructive to the relationship. Being active also means you will patiently try to fill in the blanks of your child's communication and attempt to interpret what she is saying. It is essential to recognize she is in the process of developing mature thought and language patterns, and she will need help in this maturation process. At times, you can repeat what you have heard to ensure hearing the intended message. Since you are not a mind reader, you may need to ask questions and clarify.

As you listen, clear your mind of distractions; if you cannot, you may need to postpone the interaction. Notice when your mood might be getting in the way, or if you are thinking of other things. Notice your own sense of wanting to hear what is being said. Clearly, you must take "response-ability" for your interest and participation in the communication process. Active listening is the essence of communication. As a parent, you are the role model to teach this vital communication skill.

13. HANDLING CRITICISM.

Let's face it: people have a hard time handling criticism. In fact, there is a very good book by Mary Lynne Heldman[8] entitled; *WHEN WORDS HURT; How to Keep Criticism From Undermining Your Self-Esteem.* She has three points I would like to borrow. The first is that words sometimes hurt, and I have already given you my thoughts about this. The second is that in most of our childhoods, criticism was often followed by punishment. As children, most of us felt the pain of being criticized, and the punishment deepened the pain. Naturally, punishment resulted in feelings of guilt, anxiety, hurt and isolation. From experiential learning, criticism became associated with these feelings. These childhood associations can be quite powerful in our daily lives and make it difficult to hear observations. Heldman's third point is that people tend to respond to criticism with what she refers to as the four don'ts: "defend, deny, counterattack, and withdraw." Of course, these responses avoid handling or facing our own difficult feelings.

Criticism is a part of our daily lives. It may be constructive or it may be destructive. Destructive criticism is that which is intended to hurt someone's growth process. Harsh words, name-calling, excessive expectations, manipulation, and lack of respect are aspects of destructive criticism. Constructive criticism is that which is intended to help and enhance someone's growth process. Consider how your own words would feel to you. Are they words that encourage, provide balanced observations, and allow you to find a process to feel good about changing? Are you as interested in your child's process of developing as you are in wanting your child to change? Someone told me many years ago about the following technique: Think of your child or your spouse as a business partner whom you care about. How would you provide criticism to this person? You can do this by being positive, factual, concerned about the relationship, and by using "I" messages. As you can see, this is no different than any of the other relationship-enhancing ideas.

In offering ways for you to handle criticism, I would again like to borrow some points from Mary Lynne Heldman's book. She suggests that you look at the motivation of the person giving the criticism. Is their intent positive or negative? She suggests examining your feelings and listening very carefully to the other person as well as to yourself. If you need some time to think, please take this time. As you practice this, you will become more adept at knowing whether the other person has positive or negative intentions. If they have positive intentions, you can then accept their words for consideration and respond in either a neutral or positive fashion. If they are being negative, you can agree with part of their criticism, you can suggest they might be "right," or you can suggest that you have a different opinion. With some people, you may even need to have a confrontation about your sense of their intentions. With others, you might just sidestep their negativity. If you feel bad when people continue to criticize you negatively, try not to feel guilty or ashamed about this feeling. Your reality is that when people treat you in destructive ways, you will have negative reactions. It is in your best interest to pay attention to these reactions.

Up to this point, I have been mostly concerned with handling destructive criticism. I hope you will have a much easier time with constructive criticism. Know, however, that with constructive criticism, you may still have some ill feelings. There are not many people who like hearing criticism, and it is so easy to become defensive. If your ill feelings are strong, they probably stem from events in your childhood. You may wish to use these ill feelings to delve into your memories. With constructive criticism, it is important for you to listen to the words used, weigh the motivation of the speaker, and to then consider the possible merit of the criticism. If you can view constructive criticism as enhancing positive change, the criticism can be more than beneficial. With time and practice, you may even become mildly eager to receive constructive criticism.

NOTE: These words were meant for you to receive the input of others in an open fashion. However, if someone is meddling for selfish reasons, you are certainly encouraged to confront or ignore this meddlesome input.

14. <u>INTERVENE, WHEN NECESSARY, IN YOUR CHILD'S COMMUNICATION</u>.

I have strongly advocated encouraging and listening to your child so she might feel she has a voice. This is important in her ability to state what she thinks and feels. In encouraging her to have her own voice, it is possible her voice might assume too much power; that is, she might take on the "role" of a parent. Children, sometimes, have a tendency to get "carried away" in expressing their wants or in the way they see things. Sometimes, this can be to the point of being disrespectful or to try more authority than they really have. Under these circumstances, you might provide factual observations of her communication, or you might simply assert your sense of difficulty with the communication. You may find yourself overreacting at times. It is important that you continue to model respectfulness and balance. This is the centeredness of your real personal power.

Your balanced intervention is also necessary when intense emotionality results in communication getting out of hand. This can be a nightmare without proper direction. If you remember, your child is developing, and it is your job to teach her acceptable outlets for her emotionality. This includes respectful communication. When her emotionality seems to be a hindrance to communication, you can do one of two things. The first is to wait until she calms down on her own, or after awhile, respectfully ask her to calm down so you can talk. Remember, you want effective communication; you do not want to squash her feelings. You may have to leave her presence for a bit while she, and possibly you, regain composure. Some people advocate asking children to go to their room. As a last resort, this might be necessary. However, you want to try to reach a solution as quickly as possible and through cooperation. From this angle, sending her away really is a last resort.

The second course of action is to think about and interpret her feelings, knowing that you are guessing about what is going on with her. For example, when she is being very difficult, you might say, "Maybe you are mad at something, and you are giving me your anger." Another example: she is crying, and you know her teacher fussed at her during the day. You could use this as an opportunity to ask if her feelings were hurt during the fussing or if she was upset about something in the here and now. These questions and possible interpretations provide guidance for your child to explore her own feelings. This interpreting and communicating allows you to talk to your child's inner self. You cannot be overly forceful with this, though. If you are, your child could either withdraw or fight with you by being silent. As with any rule, there may be an exception when you need to be forceful. I urge you to be cautious with forcefulness.

In summary, I encourage you to listen carefully to your child's emotional expressions. Please let her cry and be angry as long as she is communicating in a nondestructive way. When and if it goes too far, please use some form of respectful intervention. Otherwise, she may "learn" that you are unwilling to teach constructive interactive skills or that she is "bad." She can become overwhelmed with power if she is allowed to be disrespectful and to deny the mutuality of the relationship.

15. <u>PUTTING IT ALL TOGETHER</u>.

Communication is a word often used in our culture. This is the information exchanged between individuals and the information exchanged within an individual among her basic parts. At the beginning of this chapter, I suggested that the quality of our communication is dependent on the accuracy of our knowledge of ourselves. So many of us do not listen to what we really feel and know in our heart of hearts. Consequently, some, if not a lot, of our exchanged information is biased by our distortions, denial, and attempts to please. This bias is a symptom of our having a "deficit" in accepting what we really think and what we really feel. Without clear self knowledge, we can not have real empathy. Without empathy, our communication suffers. So, communication starts with knowing what you know and knowing what you don't know. This includes your real feelings and **not what you were taught to feel**. Your ability to communicate does reflect your sense of self-esteem.

Clearly, the best guideline for communication is to wonder how your words would feel if someone else were saying them. You may also wonder how easy it is for you to speak and to what degree you can communicate in a balanced fashion. In summary, I feel you need to be attentive to yourself and others. I believe your communication needs to be concise and your words must accurately reflect your message. Please attempt to set the stage so that you will be heard. It is important for your behavior to reflect what you say with words. It is important that your words reflect what you say in your behavior. Otherwise you will be communicating a lie. With this struggle, you will minimize the differences between what you say and what you do. Your image and your reality just might come very close to being the same. **What a wonderful gift to give your child and yourself!**

The following quote is another way of saying this:

"All that we do and say communicates what we feel and believe. And interestingly enough, how we communicate deeply influences how we feel."[9]

PLEASE REMEMBER: **If your children cannot talk to you, who can they talk to?** I believe that we need to do everything possible so that our children can talk to us.

133

Chapter 6

EMOTIONALITY

In A Moment Of Enlightenment I Saw At Last How I Must Appear To My Children: Kind, Quiet, Friendly-But Never Revealing Myself In Depth, Buttoning Up All My Deepest Feelings And Unconsciously Encouraging Them All To Participate In My Emotionally Maimed Charade."[1]

There are several ways to "talk" about emotionality. One is to speak about my own sense of emotionality, and another is to tell you about the journey of one of my "clients" (I really prefer the term "partner" on a psychological journey). I believe these two stories will help you understand the importance of emotions. As I do this, I quickly and fully realize the inadequacy of words. Words just do not reflect the depth of emotional experience.

It is a lot like going to a movie and not allowing yourself to get into the movie. However, words can point toward emotional depth—to reflect the power and the extent of your emotional experience. This is like when you are fully into a movie, there is no separation between self and the movie. You are really present.

I would like to be brave and share my sense of emotionality. I grew up as a fairly successful child, an achiever. I did well in school and participated in a variety of sandlot sports. However, when I started Little League Baseball, I found myself afraid I might contribute to the loss of games. I was also afraid of what my peers would think of my ability to play. The more I was afraid, the more I struck out and made errors on the field. I was on a downward spiral and did not go back to Little League. However, my dreams of playing sports did not dwindle. I was more concerned with achieving than with my fears. I would practice some with my father, and I would practice a lot by myself. At one level, I was afraid of failing, and at another, I wanted to compete successfully.

I was a small child but quite tough. I had a reputation for being able to handle pain. No one knew how scared and frightened I was. I continued to do well in school and associated with other boys who did well. I went on to high school and despite doing well academically, I felt like an outsider. I was afraid to participate in football, and I felt left out. It was clear to me that athletics were the key to success. I began wrestling, cross-country running, and tennis.

Gradually, I either felt more popular, or maybe I became more popular. I still am not sure. Despite the change in my status, I continued to be quite afraid of rejection and did not feel "good enough." I went on to college, and after great difficulty in college, I found psychology. By now, you can guess why I chose psychology.

After graduation, I was drafted into the Army and was profoundly frightened as I went through boot camp. Interestingly, I somehow knew I would not be sent to Viet Nam, and I wasn't. About two years later, I applied to one graduate school (only one, out of fear) and was accepted. Again, the fear of failure surfaced and was so overwhelming that, on occasion, I would wake up screaming in a closet, not knowing how I got there. However, I again surprised myself and did well. There was such a contrast between what I could do and what I feared I could not do. Later, I graduated and went into a deep depression. What other goal was there to keep me frightened? What goal might distract from my fear? I now had a Ph. D., but no idea of who I was or what I wanted.

I finally had to go on my own psychological journey—to explore why I was so frightened, why I could not cry, and why I did not feel my feelings. As I did this, many ordinary experiences took on new meaning; for example, socializing became exciting and I felt the phrase "I'm glad to see you." Contact with people took on a whole new meaning as I experienced others. Looking at and "feeling" trees became an enlivening experience. Breathing became important to me; I recognized it as a source of inspiration. Dreams were teaching me all sorts of valuable lessons. I started playing racquetball and learned that I could play for fun instead of success. As I became more aware, it occurred to me that while I was very successful, I felt I did not **deserve** to win. This realization allowed me a further step on my journey—a big one.

The fear went so deep that it interfered with relationships, and it interfered with my work. I had hidden my inner turmoil quite well, but it still lurked in both my conscious and unconscious experiences. As I learned to be open to this fear, I became open to much of the pain I had been withholding. I stopped blaming myself and others. Understanding and openness to all my feelings bestowed great freedom.

I am grateful for my psychological journey into my real self. I am grateful for the aliveness that my emotionality has brought me. From this experience, I know for certain that emotionality can be destructive, or it can set me free. I have learned that my self-esteem must come from inside myself and not just from my achievements. Success does not bring long term happiness. It just looks that way. While I was profoundly frightened throughout much of my life, I now accept most of this fear. As I accept it, and as I work with my fear, I am also overcoming this age-old obstacle.

It is important for you to know that even now I can be scared and feel insecure. The difference is I am now conscious of this and know how to deal with those remaining fears and insecurities. I no longer have to change something or "fix" something when I feel these feelings. Being alive, I will continue to have all sorts of feelings. I can use the pain as well as the joy to benefit myself and others. Hopefully, I will use my feelings constructively; that is my intent.

In my work with psychological partners, the issue of fear is almost always present, as it was present for me. They, along with myself, had difficulties with feeling worthy and whole. You may be wondering about this fear, and I have some correlative observations. Of course, these observations relate to how we do and do not relate to our insides.

In our families and in our culture, there is an extreme emphasis on what we wear, what we have, and what we do. We notice how quickly our children walk, talk, say their first sentences, dress, behave, participate in school, and so on. As I said in the beginning, we have a tendency to emphasize concrete goals and de-emphasize the process of achieving these goals. As a result, our children tend to focus on achievement or lack thereof. There is a good side to this; there is a need for us to be productive human beings. There is also a bad side; many of us are fearful of not achieving enough. We then either concentrate heavily on concrete success or become paralyzed with fear.

In some cases, I, for example, carried both an emphasis on success and inside a fear of failure. Because I was so focused on achievement, I felt unworthy. In other words, I was unconscious of the fact that I was loved. As a result, I devoted my life to "proofs" of my worthiness through achievement. On the inside, I was so afraid of others' disapproval that I was paralyzed. This paralysis affected my ability to feel my feelings, express my feelings, or to speak in front of a group. I took a speech class in college and was so anxious, I was nauseous.

I feel quite thankful, at one level, for my concentration on success. At another level, I wish there had been individuals who could have spoken to my fear. My **fantasy** is that I would then have understood my desire for success and brought my fear into balance. It is for these reasons that we need to balance our emphasis on achievement with the emotional and spiritual sides of life. This has been my purpose as a psychologist, not just for others, but for myself.

The following quote highlights the struggle that many people endure: "I am tired of proving to the world that I am not as bad as I feel."[2]

I would now like to offer, with her permission, a story from a partner's psychological journey. As she grew up, her eyes required a lot of medical attention. This struggle with her eyes gave her a profound sense of nonacceptance. Although she had been thin during most of her childhood, she later became obsessed with eating. She joined a support group and her weight went up and down. As she initiated her psychological journey, she began to realize she could not tolerate sadness, anger, or any psychological pain; she would either eat or withdraw.

She began to have dreams of men hurting her, and she was able to fend off these men in her dreams. She would have dreams of being frightened by many strange people being in her house. She dreamed of being overwhelmed by high waves of water; however, she emerged unscathed from each of these dreams.

Later in her journey, she had a "real life," eye-opening experience. One day she was leading a meeting, feeling very anxious and dry-mouthed. She was experiencing difficulty in speaking, so she took a break. During the break, she could not decide whether or not to go back before the group. She also debated whether or not she would tell the group what had happened. She decided to share her sense of anxiety—her fear of being "seen." This allowed the group to see her in the depth of her fear and her tears. This allowed them to be with her and nurture her openness. She then understood, along with the group, that food was a substitute for cherishing her inner-most feelings. This openness to her inner being has given her freedom to live life more fully.

I hope these two portrayals reveal to you the power of emotionality. Your emotions can work for you, or they can work against you. The "trick" is to identify the factors, past and present, that hinder or free the flow of your emotions. For your own benefit, you need to fully understand how your feelings operate. As a culture, we need to understand the emotional needs of ourselves and our children. As you continue reading, I would like you to consider the following question: **"Can you know your child without knowing and understanding how she feels?"**

1. EMOTIONALITY IS AN INTERNAL EXPERIENCE.

As are all human beings, your child was born with the capacity to experience and reveal any number of emotions. These feelings and responses become more varied and recognizable with age. Initially, babies can display two or three emotional states. With age and experience the number and complexity of these states increases to as many as ten to fifteen. Your child senses and knows these emotional states as an internal experience. From this internal experience, she may display any number of external reactions (seen on the outside). These will either reveal or hide what is occurring on the inside. Your child can be quite expressive with these internal reactions, and she can find many constructive ways to release these feelings. Her feelings can serve her well unless she is taught otherwise.

From my viewpoint, feelings are the internal energies which flow out of her life spirit—her soul. This flowing of internal energy gives her the experience of life. As a result, these internal responses are the essence of your child's real self, her sense of life. This life spirit, or soul, is the part of your child I refer to as her "core being." When a child is taught to keep her internal reactions to herself, she learns to hide her life spirit. She learns that this core is somehow bad or not to be seen. This creates deep level self-esteem problems. This teaching pushes a child to "forget" or not acknowledge the deepest level of her insides.

This child will then ignore and deny the energy flowing from her spirit. After a while, this denial will come more easily; it becomes a habit. As the habit increases, the greater the deadness she will experience. As this deepens, she will feel unworthy, unlovable, and unacceptable.

This deadening is at the center of my version of craziness. Deadening of a child's spirit is mean, denying, and typically is masked with a culturally acceptable story. Drugs or other artificially enlivening experiences create a mask to hide the deadness. These deadening and masking processes are so powerful they can become addictive and unconscious. To prevent this deadening, we need an atmosphere which encourages the constructive expression of our internal energies.

I do not believe you would want to deaden your child. Consequently, you need to be conscious of the pressures to minimize feeling experiences. You can be an agent to counteract these pressures. Family can then become a safe place for emotionality and spirit.

139

2. EMOTIONALITY IS THE HUMAN THERMOSTAT.

While this idea is simplistic, it serves as a clear, mental image for the usefulness of feelings. Feelings indicate the state of your insides just as a thermostat tells you about the temperature inside your house. With this information, you can make decisions in response to how you feel. Your house thermostat makes decisions about heating and cooling, depending on how it is programmed. Like other human beings, your past experience has you programmed to do certain things with your emotions. It is quite likely your feelings and behavior interact in "preset" ways. However (thank goodness), as a human being, you are capable of learning how to change your program. Changing your program is not easy, and sometimes requires outside help. With awareness and dedication, you and others can make very different decisions about what happens internally and externally. You may then pass on these new responses to your children.

3. EMPHASIZE EMOTIONAL LANGUAGE.

Children are aware of which subjects may be discussed and which are taboo. Your openly speaking about feelings gives you and your child permission to speak and feel in an open manner. Certain groups are concerned that there is already too much permission to speak openly. In some areas, they might be correct. However, forcing a child's feelings underground denies a child the tools to deal with that part of her. Again, this deadens, and I hope I have made my point about the consequences of deadening.

There is a middle ground: allow her to feel freely while teaching the constructive use of her insides. She needs to know that feelings, by themselves, are harmless and need to be freely experienced. She will need help in developing a language to identify feelings. You can concentrate on the emotional process by using words that identify the various emotional reactions. Begin simplistically by using "mad, sad, scared, and glad (or happy)." As your child matures, you can use more complicated words such as "disappointed, frustrated, anxious, helpless," and so on. However, the basics of "mad, sad, scared, and glad" will continue to serve you well. This emphasis

140

will encourage her to be more open as she identifies the feeling process and understands what is occurring within her.

4. THERE IS A DIFFERENCE BETWEEN EMOTIONAL BEING AND DOING.

In this culture, there appears to be a fear of intense emotions. If my perception is correct, this fear is of the wrong thing and is misdirected. Intense emotions do not hurt other people. If you look carefully at strong emotions, they are nothing more than an intense state of emotional being. From this emotional state, **you can choose to act** in any number of ways, either constructively or destructively. Some people do choose to "act out" their emotions in such a way they hurt themselves or someone else. Yes, this is destructive, and it does have an emotional basis. However, prohibiting or deadening a feeling does not stop emotional or physical injury. The fact is that people hurt; your child has and will hurt; and our culture is hurting.

It is of greater value to encourage people both to be aware of their feelings and to notice what they do with these feelings. In this way, feelings are not "bottled up" and, therefore, cannot become explosive. With this awareness and permission, feelings are then released constructively. Intense feelings can be quite painful, but if you are really going to become "strong," you will let these feelings pass through in constructive ways. Being "strong" does not mean covering your insides at the expense of your wholeness. Being "strong" is balancing constructive interactions with your emotional experiences.

As a side note, there are many who think that people should just forget the hurts of their past and present. They see this as a necessary step toward picking up the pieces and moving into the future. Part of the process is then overlooked and these feelings are then suppressed (made unconscious). As a result, forgetting the past is a type of band-aid. Fortunately, a recent study supports positive change from telling one's story. "Keeping thoughts secret creates a suppression cycle."[3] From experience, you may already know this.

Another common concern is the sense of being out of control while experiencing intense feelings. Many individuals report that they feel out of control when they experience their feelings. This is a correct reporting during moments where feelings are the primary determinant of our experience. In these moments, our emotional energies are surging from the spirit. This is an "out of control" experience. As a result, it is difficult, if not impossible, to control our feelings. This may frighten you. Remember, though, this is a state of emotional **being** that will pass.

There is an alternative, moreover, that transforms this "out of control" experience into a constructive one. As human beings, we can operate at more than one level at a time. Instead of deadening these strong experiences, the mind can monitor how they are being felt physically, how they are expressed, and the consequences. Very simply, you can use your mind to register what you are doing with your feelings. Thus, you can be out of control, in a manner of speaking, and yet control what these energies do. You can do this by experiencing intense feelings and letting yourself monitor the behavior and thinking that occurs. This is awareness. From this monitoring, you can know that you are expressing your feelings constructively. As long as no destructive behavior occurs, you have experienced the intense feelings, allowed the energy to run its course, and found a way to release the energy constructively. From this, you can eventually, if not quickly, return to a state of "finished" calm.

This is like skiing; you can flow with the skiing, but you can also stop or turn whenever you choose. Another useful example is the out of control experience you can have with intense, sexual feelings. For many people, these are a delight, and, for others, scary. Here too, it is possible to control what you do with the feelings, and how they flow through you. In general, it is possible with practice to be in control while you are out of control.

5. <u>FEELINGS AND WHOLENESS</u>.

If you will remember from Chapter 2, each of us behaves, thinks, feels, and has a spirit. High self-esteem and wholeness come from these four parts working well together. This also comes from a resolution of past exeriences, so that you have very little "unfinished business." The opposite of wholeness (being split) comes with blocking.

There are three ways that blocking "gets in the way" of wholeness. To begin with, when humans block, they tend to generalize. That is, they tend to block more than just the "painful" experience. For example, someone who blocks her grieving for a loved one may also find herself avoiding people, places, clothing, aromas, or music that remind her of the loved one. This avoidance is deadening and is the essence of depression. That is, when people block, they depress the feelings and the thoughts which accompany the experience. With this blocking, there is likely to be a sense that part of their very being is either missing or disturbed. From a psychological perspective, this is true.

A second way blocking interferes with wholeness is quite prevalent. This blocking comes from the idea that humans are supposed to be a certain way if they are going to be "good" people. "Good" people are supposed to be happy, joyful, positive, and content. Projecting this "good" illusion deadens the alive experience and prohibits conversation about one's true reality.

True reality is when life brings difficult situations. We then experience a different set of emotional responses. Difficult experiences bring up pain (eg. sadness, anger, jealousy), which our culture views as negative. At the same time, there is a natural tendency for people to avoid negative feelings, but they are avoiding the wrong thing. The negative feelings are the natural accompaniment of the negative experience; that is, the feelings go with the territory. Experiencing the negative feelings constructively allows a release and minimizes the scarring.

The third way is in terms of "unfinished business." As you know, "unfinished business" refers to something which has occurred that you did not fully experience. By not fully experiencing an incident, it then becomes blocked emotional energy. As a way of demonstrating, let me give you an experience. Think of something (eg. a pink elephant), and then tell yourself not to think of that something. Or try to tell yourself not to think at all. What happens?

Blocking actually increases the energy level of the thoughts or feelings you are trying to block. This energy usually occurs at the unconscious level and can affect you when you least expect it. This is why people often say things or do things they later regret. When thoughts or feelings of earlier incidents are blocked, they tend to take on a very large energy source. Consequently, blocking interferes with your parts working well together; it prevents wholeness. People block because they "see" negative energy and for one reason or another, they do not want to feel. Generally, society considers feelings of sadness, anger, anxiety, and jealousy as feelings to be avoided or even shameful. I would like to show you how these feelings can be used to enhance your wholeness.

A. SADNESS

I am beginning with sadness because I believe it has the most impact of all the feelings; sadness has come to play a very powerful role in my life. As a male, I had a very difficult time with crying, and I used anger to cover-up my sadness. Substituting anger for sadness gave me an unnecessary hardness and lessened the intensity of my other feelings. Consequently, I knew I was not "in touch" with my true self. It was hard to trust my feelings.

I am aware that I have used my pain destructively. I have been destructive to both myself and to others. In the process of sorting this out, I have become aware of my confusion between the pain and the incidents that caused the pain. Sorting and "touching" the sadness has made me less destructive. My sadness has added to the softness and fullness of my life.

With this in mind, I do not believe it is in the culture's best interest to deny the culture's feelings of loss and suffering. This denial is crazy and portrays the world as a storybook fantasy. Acknowledging and experiencing cultural sadness would encourage a cultural connection.

Pain also comes with the loss of experience. While people are familiar with the loss of someone or something of value, they do not seem to be as familiar with the loss of experience. A major reason for this lack of familiarity is that the loss of experience is not as obvious as the loss of a loved one or object. Let me give you two examples of how this may occur in children.

The first example is of a child who grows up in a home in

144

which there is an absence of emotional affection. Consciously, the child may not know there is an absence of affection, because she does not have the experience of having had it. However, this same child is likely to notice a vague feeling that something is wrong or that something is missing. She will then either dismiss the feeling or try to find ways to get rid of the feeling. Later on, as she becomes conscious of her loss of affection, she will then experience the accompanying pain. A second example is of a child who wants more time and attention from her father. At first, the child might experience the pain of missing her father, but she will get "used to" his not being very available. As she gets used to this, she will become unconscious of the loss of time and attention. However, her entire being is affected by this loss. In fact, this change in being can create serious relationship problems for her later in life.

Unfortunately, there is a large group of people who believe that sadness or pain is a sign of weakness or vulnerability. This is not necessarily so. However, if someone collapses, gives up, allows themselves to be manipulated, or refuses to function, they have succumbed to their pain. In these instances, an individual is not allowing the pain to create aliveness. They are either succumbing or deadening.

On the other hand, there are situations where the pain is so great that a person is quite likely to feel overwhelmed and helpless. In many instances, such as a death, this is indeed reality. If you do what society **generally** suggests, you will be strong on these occasions and not admit to helplessness. Or you might try to minimize the feelings that go with helplessness. If you will remember the loss of the family dog (from the third chapter), the "strong" reaction would have been for me to have kept a stiff upper lip, acted as if dogs were not very important, and not cried over a dead dog. Of course, there was nothing I could do about the loss of our dog. Thankfully, I learned from this experience.

Sadness is an intensely powerful feeling. It literally can take over. You feel sad, cry, or even sob. Sadness is meant to be shared. It can draw you closer to others, and this sharing usually leads to a lessening of the pain. Sharing the sadness can help others to learn

145

from you. Allowing your sadness increases contact with your experience as well as your inner self. As your inner self strengthens, you will have additional support for processing the rest of your unfinished experience. Allowing sadness encourages experiencing all of your parts.

B. ANGER

Anger appears to be the most frequently expressed negative feeling. It is a common feeling when someone does not like something, does not get his/her way, is being treated badly, senses coercion, or is threatened. Maybe anger is too widely accepted or valued; I just don't know. I am struck with there being so much angry talk and with there being a "war" on just about everything. I'm also aware of how often people are verbally or physically abused if they do not think a certain way. On the other hand, many people are afraid of their anger and have a hard time expressing it constructively.

In feeling angry, people report intense energy stirring around inside, a desire to strike out, an explosiveness, or a desire to get even. As is the case with sadness, this feeling needs to be released so that a sense of wholeness can be restored. However, since anger has more potential to be destructive, its release must be carefully considered.

Probably the most constructive choice is to talk about the anger using "I" phrases. Not in an aggressive way, but in a way that conveys why and how you feel. For example, you might say "I am angry; I have asked you three times to take out the garbage." Or you might tell your spouse you are angry about his/her preoccupation with other things. "I am angry" gives a message that can be talked about and respectful talking often relieves most or all of the anger. If both of you are good-willed, the two of you will work out differences to the benefit of the relationship.

However, if the other person is not cooperative, you may have to find substitute ways of releasing this angry energy. Please remember that anger is experienced in the form of energy, and, until you release the energy, you will have a sense of being unfinished. Otherwise, you will be prone to irritation, frustration, angry outbursts, depression, or sadness. Healthy substitutes are physical releases such as tennis, running, racquetball, hitting pillows, crying, or any other activity in which you have an image that goes with the angry energy. This allows you to feel a deep release. It may also lead you to a deep sense of loss that fuels anger.

This may sound stupid to you. If it does, it may be that you have learned that emotional energy is bad, emotional energy is to be hidden, or to be very self-conscious. If any of these are true, please consider how you will allow yourself to be more emotionally expressive. You may then find the emotional expression with which you are most comfortable.

To find your sense of release, you might think about what the angry energy would "most like to do" that would not hurt anyone. The trick is to listen to the energy and let what you hear guide your choice. By using your mind to monitor how the energy is coming out, you can remain in control while releasing the energy. This is clearly better than being verbally disrespectful or punching someone. **It is sad and scary that so many people do not feel satisfied until they hit or hurt someone.**

Anger is certainly a necessary energy. It often leads us to take constructive, positive, action—to do what needs to be done. Constructively, it is energy that can lead to positive action. Be open to talking about your anger in respectful ways and find substitutes for striking people. Please remember angry, disrespectful words can be the psychological equivalent of hitting people. Angry words used in a respectful manner can be the key to more intimacy. You may use this as a model for teaching your child to be appropriately and respectfully angry when she needs to be. This will also allow her to be soft when she needs to be.

I fully realize that the above words are more easily said than done. To be respectful and to be angry may seem a contradiction in terms. It is helpful to remember that you do have a soft, tender side that can be hurt. Many people substitute anger for their sense of pain. If you can balance this softness with the tendency to "strike out," your response will be much more constructive.

Since handling anger is so difficult, I would like to talk about two situations and provide some ideas about handling the anger re-

147

spectfully. The first example relates to your child continuing to bounce a ball after being asked to come to dinner. Please imagine your feelings with being "ignored," "rejected," or possibly "defied." Imagine what you would usually say and do in this type of situation. What is the first thing that "wants" to come out of your mouth?

Now, let me suggest some possibilities. First, "Have you heard me ask you to come to dinner?" Second, "Do you realize what it is like when you do not come to dinner?" Third, "I'm feeling angry you do not seem to be listening. Is there a problem?" Fourth, "Would you like to help in choosing a dinner time that would be convenient for both you and the rest of the family?" And if your attempts at mutuality are failing, you might raise your voice and say, "I don't understand your problem in listening to me!" The intent of this statement is to get your child's attention so that there might be a discussion. I realize there are moments when respectful attempts fail, and I encourage you to set limits subsequent to failure. In this case, you might use the natural consequence of asking her to take the ball elsewhere while you eat without her. This is not harsh in light of your respectful attempts.

The second example demonstrates a way of handling potential conflict between you and your spouse (this is good for modeling respectful behavior). Your spouse has asked you to take a special vacation, and you find the requested vacation time has been taken by a co-worker. You feel angry and somewhat sad that your vacation hopes have been dashed. What would you normally say about your anger and sadness? Here are some possiblities. You could say something as simple as "I'm angry that my vacation time has been taken by a co-worker; can we find another week?" Or you might say, "I am sorry about the time conflict; could we use the time another way?" Or you might say, "I can only imagine how you must feel; can we discuss your feelings?" You might say all of the above and add to it whatever fits your experience. Notice the "I" messages, the feeling words, the words oriented toward the conflict, and the respectfulness of the words.

On your first reading of these words, you might be quite skeptical of your ability to say these kinds of things, or you might be skeptical of the words themselves. Generally, this is not the way our culture talks when angry. However, if you concentrate on your balance, your love, and your spirituality, you will find your anger can become quite balanced and respectful. **It is imperative for our children to learn constructive ways to handle anger.**

C. ANXIETY

Anxiety is often considered to be negative. Actually, it is only negative in that it signals when something is not quite right or whole, or when there is a danger. There is a disturbance, and the feeling signals the disturbance. The disturbance is negative, not the feeling. The feeling is a positive communication of disturbance.

To use the anxiety constructively, you must first consider its reasons for being. Have you been exposed to serious threats, or have your feelings been hurt? Maybe you feel that an endearing relationship is in danger. Maybe you are concerned about how well you are going to do on a certain task. In this sense, anxiety is a signal that tells you something needs to be explored. I would suggest that you explore the meaning of your anxiety and attempt a resolution. If the anxiety is overwhelming, you may need to lessen the anxiety with relaxation or other adjunctive therapies while you complete your exploration. (Please see the discussion at the end of this chapter for extreme cases of anxiety.)

From a psychological view, anxiety has a very strong potential usefulness. Anxiety often indicates internal conflict, which simply means that one part of you is in conflict with another part of you. For example, one part may want to be loving with your child, and another part creates anger over trivial incidents. As another example, one part of you may want to say something, and another part is afraid of a negative reaction. As long as you do not resolve these conflicts, you are likely to experience anxiety.

Anxiety arises when a person either does not know who they are or they are unable to be themselves (to be what they know they are capable of being). In other words, anxiety occurs when a person is inhibited to let an inner part (or parts) of himself be seen. There is anxiety over one' true self being seen. It could be that a person is afraid to see or is afraid that others might see. These are learned reactions.

Another form of internal conflict arises when unreleased emotional energy remains from past events. I have previously used the term "unfinished business" to refer to this. Clearly, anxiety in the form of "unfinished business" is a signal to take positive action by working with this emotional energy.

I hope this allows you to see anxiety differently. It is an energy, and it is present only if there is a reason. You may use this energy constructively by exploring it and wondering if certain parts of yourself might be in conflict. You may then pursue resolving internal conflicts and unfinished business. If your child shows excessive anxiety or enough anxiety to concern you, I would strongly suggest that you obtain professional guidance.

D. JEALOUSY

Jealousy is often referred to as the "green-eyed monster." As with all feelings, the experience of jealousy can be either constructive or destructive, depending on which behavior arises from this feeling. First, what does the word mean? In its usual sense, it means you have an ill feeling because someone else has something that you want. You might want that something, or you might be angry with the person who has it. Basically, you are upset because you do not have that something. As a result, there is a resentment. This can be accompanied by an increased awareness of what you do not have or an increased awareness of what the other person has. This is a form of vigilance and can turn into suspicion and mistrust. At this level, the green-eyed monster can be quite powerful. Obviously, this is destructive, and many destructive behaviors can come from this feeling. For example, "cutting another person down" is quite destructive. Expending great personal energy to monitor who gets more than you would also be destructive.

On the other hand, jealousy can be constructive if used properly. From time to time, people are going to notice what others have and wish for more. This, in and of itself, is fairly normal. If it passes without any destructive behavior, it is of no concern. If it does not pass quickly, you can then use your jealousy to explore its origins. For example, it may come from a psychological hunger resulting from a sense of deprivation. Or it may come from being unfavorably compared to others, giving you the feeling that you are an "underdog." Only through this exploration, analysis, and subsequent healing of the feelings can you grow and come to peace with the reasons behind your jealousy. If you push your jealousy out of your awareness, you are likely to find yourself engaging in bitter behaviors without realizing why. It may even result in your having a resentful and unhappy demeanor.

E. SUMMARY

As you can see, and probably have experienced, these feelings are quite difficult to express in our culture. These feelings are usually thought of as negative. Of course, pain is thought to be negative. But these feelings are a part of your being in this world; they are a part of your sense of wholeness. Wholeness is clearly affected by whether or not you block your feelings. Wholeness is clearly affected by whether or not you allow your feelings to take you to constructive completion. When blocked, these feelings move into the unconscious where they can push you to do things you ordinarily would not do. When you depress these so-called negative feelings, you are depressing your aliveness. You are depressing your wholeness. Using these feelings destructively does not help you or anyone else. Conscious effort is required to monitor how you feel, as well as how you give constructive expression to these feelings. You can incorporate this conscious effort into your being and thus teach it, by example, to your children. The following quote provides inspiration for your feeling journey:

"What we have in the present is feeling, and the feeling is difficult and uncomfortable. If we engage that feeling without rejection, without trying to change it, psychologically explain or label it, we can come to true acceptance. When a feeling is finally accepted it doesn't capture our attention

151

any more and is not respressed. We become present with the feeling, no longer reacting , trying to change, or get away from it; and all the energy inside the feeling becomes life force. We literally become more luminous. . . ."[4]

6. THE EMOTIONAL PROCESS CAN BECOME UNCONSCIOUS.

I have suggested that blocked feelings move into the unconscious, and by being unconscious, these thoughts and feelings are removed from awareness. Without awareness, these unconscious feelings and thoughts can convert into powerful energies that "slip out" when you are reminded of them. They can also "slip out" when there is no reminder at all (eg. in dreams). This energy slippage gives you surplus (extra) emotional energy or an impulse to do what you ordinarily would not do. This is often why adults overreact or cannot explain why they did something out of character. Thus, these unaware processes can play a powerful role in human lives.

Generally, the degree of unawareness can vary from a little unaware to partially unaware to greatly unaware. You might want to consider where you are on this continuum. Also, consider what it is like to be around people who are very aware versus those who are greatly unaware.

There is no doubt that young children are acutely sensitive. They may not know the why's, what's, or how's of their experiences, but they often know their reactions are strong and quick. Yet, the knowledge that their reactions are strong and quick can be somewhat hidden from themselves. As they grow, children vary in their knowledge of what happens internally.

They also vary in their willingness to notice and observe what happens internally. There appears to be two major factors affecting their willingness and ability to be aware. The first factor is something that you can influence—what you model and verbally encourage. The second is something over which you will have little control—your child's tolerance for experiencing emotions. The greater her tolerance, the more likely she will be aware. With less tolerance,

152

your child is more likely to find ways not to notice and she will divert this energy elsewhere. Of course, this is not the best way to adapt, but for some children it is the only way they know.

You may be quite concerned and frustrated if your child has adapted in this manner. It is even more difficult to understand when you try to reach her, and she blocks you. Of course, we think every child wants to be understood. Not always! As a result, your questions about the why's and wherefore's of your child may receive "I don't know's" as answers. This does not necessarily require professional consultation (see professional consultation chapter). However, if you have lost contact with your child, your family is likely to benefit from professional consultation.

7. STAY WITH YOUR CHILD'S EMOTIONALITY.

Staying with your child's emotionality means you encourage her by being present and connected as she constructively experiences her emotions. Being present and connected means allowing yourself to feel and understand the process of what she is experiencing. If you have difficulty staying with your own emotionality, you will have difficulty staying with hers. Your child's feelings may remind you of how your own feelings are blocked or of experiences which taught you to block. Your child's feelings may arouse your own painful feelings. Just experiencing your child's feelings can be quite painful.

In this culture, there is a strong tendency to divert the emotional energy away from the experience; this blocks the energy from passing through. Our culture calls this making people feel better. While this is a wonderful goal, it misses the underlying process of really helping people to feel better versus faking it with distractions.

Let me give you some examples of distractions. The first is telling your child she should be happy. This is often called "counting your blessings." While I have no quarrel with happiness or blessings, **life is not always this way!** A second distraction is giving pleasurable food in the moment of pain. A very painful third distraction is to tell a crying child you will really give her something to cry about. If you think honestly about these distractions, you'll see they are abusive. Of course, some are not as abusive as others, but they are abusive in the sense of distortion, denial, and the infliction of further pain.

Painful feelings exist. This truth is not an encouragement of unhappiness. It is an encouragement and permission to go through the process of living one's life fully. As you learn to process your own emotions, you will be able to "stay with" your child's emotional process. You can not take away her pain, but you can help her heal the wounds which accompany her pain. You can be with her and affirm her feelings as she goes through emotional experiences.

8. THERE ARE TYPICAL CHILDHOOD REACTIONS.

Many parents become upset with typical childhood reactions because they appear childish. Yes, they are childlike, and it makes sense they would be. Do not take away your child's childhood before she is ready! This does not mean being permissive; it means being balanced. When acting childish is destructive to relationships, feel free to intervene. It is one thing to be childlike; it is another to be destructive. As a quick example, your child might be jealous of her brother or sister. This is one state of being; it would be another for her to kick her sibling. Being jealous is certainly a common part of childhood. You must use your intuition and judgment about when to set limits.

There are many typical childhood reactions, such as being afraid of the dark, not wanting to go to bed, wanting to sleep with parents, avoiding work responsibilities, wanting to play, being afraid of new situations, being angry when she does not get what she wants, wanting to be first, and so on. Within reasonable boundaries, try not to worry about these reactions. For the most part, let your children be children and, in the parental role, don't be overly responsible. If you are certain her behavior is becoming destructive, intervene. Again, parenting is a real high-wire balancing act. Give yourself permission to be tolerant! Give yourself permission to set limits! Give yourself time to make choices!

9. DO NOT ENCOURAGE OR FORCE EMOTIONAL LIES.

Many people do not like to see or feel "negative" reactions. This discourages emotional honesty. I am not talking about brutal honesty, but honesty balanced with respect for other people. Your child is going to have reactions of anger, sadness, jealousy, and disappointment in situations not to her liking. To encourage or force her to be "positive" is to force her to lie. Positivism has a place, but when the price is your child's true reality, it is a lie.

If she cries, do not discourage her from crying. If your child is afraid, allow her to obtain comfort in your words and affection. If your child is angry, give her acceptable ways to allow this energy. If she is excited with happiness, do not tell her to calm down. With this support, you can guide your child to express her feelings in a constructive way while limiting any attempt to use feelings to manipulate or hurt. Do not use name-calling to set limits. Instead, communicate how she might be using her feelings destructively. Do this in a mutually beneficial way! With guidance and support for constructive expression, your child "should" return to a calm state within minutes. Larger and more lifestyle-altering events will take longer and possibly require several expressions of feelings. Generally, these expressions are referred to as natural grieving.

Momentous events such as death, divorce, or the loss of a favorite pet may normally take weeks or months to begin healing. Large events may continue their impact into adulthood. Of course, many childhood events leave their mark well into adulthood. Please remember, there are individual differences among humans, and there is no way to accurately predict how long the grieving will take place.

In the event of a significant loss, I would suggest that you monitor your child's general behavior, and, if you notice negative effects, talk again about the loss. This talking will encourage your child to express her feelings of loss; this allows her to work through left-over energies. Some children may resist this talking; you may have to be somewhat gentle (and subtle) in your encouragement. If, after three months, your child's functioning has not improved considerably, I would suggest professional consultation. If your child does not seem to be grieving over the significant loss, you might want to consider consultation before three months. The lack of grieving could reflect a general coping pattern of denial.

Of course, the best way to encourage emotional truth is for you to be a model of open and constructive emotionality. Your openness sets the atmosphere and gives permission for the experiencing and expression of feelings. Last, but not least, please remember you cannot take away your child's pain. However, you can be there as she goes through the experiences of her life.

10. BE BALANCED IN YOUR EMOTIONAL SUPPORT.

While it is important to support your child's emotionality, there can be a point when her feelings are so strong that they get in the way. When this occurs, emotionality has become destructive. You, as her parent, have the difficult task of analyzing and deciding what to do. For example, if a child strongly feels her parent loves a sibling more than her, one of three things could be occurring: 1. the child is right and the loving is different; 2. because of the differences in the children, a parent does respond differently but is relatively equal in loving each of them (as equal as possible); 3. by trying to make-up to this child, the making up reinforces the child's belief she is being treated differently. In other words, the child uses the parent's response to validate the complaint.

Giving in to the complaint under the wrong circumstances will block closeness instead of enhancing it. Parents must attempt to distinguish between a child's real feelings and her conscious or unconscious attempt to manipulate. If you notice that your child's complaint seems to intensify with your attempts to be supportive, you may be reinforcing manipulative behaviors. This does not mean that you should give up or ignore your child. You may need to add more firmness to provide a limit around expressing feelings destructively. In this manner, you limit the use of feeling to create destructive tension.

11. NOTICE OVERREACTIONS IN FAMILY EMOTIONALITY.

Children's reactions are often very intense, and you need to be careful in calling these "overreactions." As long as your child's reactions do not become destructive, allow and encourage her feelings to go into constructive expression. However, you may notice others overreacting to certain events. To evaluate this possiblility, you may observe your own emotional reactions and listen to those very carefully.

Here are examples of what I consider overreactions: a lengthy withdrawal over a minor incident, screaming at your child over a spilled drink, or spanking over a minor infraction of the rules. Dramatized and exaggerated thinking such as believing your child is a juvenile delinquent before the age of eight is also an overreaction.

Please give considerable thought to any overreactions occuring within your family. Some are easier to handle than others, and they are a part of being human. Some overreactions are very destructive, especially when they occur repeatedly. Please have the courage to evaluate the overreactions in your family with an eye toward measuring the degree of their destructive character. Then do what it takes to make corrections in these overreactions.

12. DO NOT LET EMOTIONS TURN INTO MANIPULATIONS.

Please remember, once again, emotions are feelings or internal reactions. They may feel either pleasant or unpleasant. People have a hard time with the unpleasant feelings and want to control them as a way of being strong. Artificial strength results in the suppression of feelings. Another negative use of feelings is manipulation.

Many people believe that others "make" them feel certain feelings; their feelings are "caused" by another's behavior. There are many common examples: "My child makes me mad." "You are driving me crazy." The implication is perfectly clear; if you are making me feel a certain way, then "stop it." Life is not so simple. No one can make you feel any particular feeling. However, what I do might result in your being sad, frustrated, angry, or in your avoiding me.

To maintain a mutual relationship, I must acknowledge my behavior which might have these results, and I must take responsibility (response-ability) for my behavior. At the same time, we must both realize I have not "made" you feel any particular feeling.

You will not be influenced unless there is something in you I can influence. Interaction is between two people, and both people participate. To put this another way, for me to psychologically influence you, I have to "hook" something inside of you that will allow me to influence you. That something has to be a pool of feelings vulnerable to my remarks or behavior.

A personal example of the "hooking" process might help. I am quite bald. If I had a problem with my baldness, most remarks about it would bother me. You could hook me. If I do not have any personal problems (sensitivity) with my baldness, your remarks will not "get to" (affect) me. Thus, under ordinary circumstances, you cannot make me feel bad about my baldness. In other words, there is no inner pool of feelings vulnerable to your remarks.

The function of feelings is not to make other people change their behavior. Feelings are a thermostat. With this thermostat, I may decide to change the temperature of the house, I may decide to change my clothing, or I may decide to fix the thermostat. I have lots of choices. Hopefully, I will read the thermostat accurately, and hopefully, the thermostat works accurately. I can then verbalize the reading off my thermostat.

If there is another person involved, my partner will join me in a mutual sensing of this reading. If we are partners in the interaction, we will come to a mutual decision to benefit the relationship. If we are not partners, I am going to have feelings about the lack of mutuality in this relationship. At some point, I will have to confront the lack of mutuality, and I might have to take drastic steps to change the way we handle the relationship. At the point where my partner is no longer a partner, my feelings will become a tool for change or a tool for removing myself from the relationship.

13. DO NOT LET EMOTIONS BE DESTRUCTIVE.

Up to this point, I have given a very positive picture of feelings. I did this to counteract the negative view of so many people. However, as with all good things, there can be a destructive side to feelings, a side that can create very grave difficulties for some people. Two main types of emotional difficulties may develop. One is that you might become so emotional you lose sight completely of how you affect others. From this loss you could then destroy the balance between the fulfillment of your needs and the needs of those you love. The other is that you could become so emotional you lose track of what your mind is telling you. This is destructive when your feelings are overreactions, when you lose your sense of purpose, when you become excessively helpless, or when you are abusive. In the extreme, you could completely lose touch with reality. There needs to be a balance or an integration between your mind and emotions. I would like to offer some examples in which feelings have become destructive. The intensity of these examples can range from mild to quite severe.

A. Anxiety, as I stated earlier, can lead to useful exploration or it can lead to difficulties. One form of anxiety occurs when a person has the feeling of fear in the absence of any concrete evidence that something bad is going to happen. This anxiety might become so severe that a person thinks others are out to hurt him/her (sometimes this is true), or a person might have panic attacks. Anxiety can come from a fear of death. Most people have some anxiety about dying, but it can become a preoccupation. Unless there is a serious illness, this probably has gone too far. A milder version of anxiety is nervousness. Some people do not feel them differently. Either way, anxiety and nervousness are uncomfortable feelings that need exploration. Extreme or overwhelming forms of anxiety typically require medication and relaxation techniques to provide relief.

B. Post-traumatic stress disorders can occur when an individual has experienced a very disturbing event or a series of disturbing events. Afterwards, this individual may experience anxiety, memories of the event, and possibly difficulties with everyday functioning such as sleeping, eating and so on. In my opinion, these disorders are fairly common, whether mild or serious. There are many cues which remind people of earlier, disturbing events.

C. Depression occurs when a person is depressing (or suppressing) their aliveness and has lowered energy levels. Depression may occur for a variety of reasons, both physical and psychological. Seriously depressed people lose the desire to keep trying and have a prolonged sense of helplessness. Often, seriously depressed individuals describe themselves as helpless and hopeless. These feelings can occur in milder form. Depression can occur suddenly, or it can be present over a long period of time. Depression can interfere with everyday activities such as job performance, eating and sleeping. Depression can be treated psychologically when mild to moderate, and probably requires medication when severe. Depression is quite common in our culture.

D. The opposite of depression is mania or an extremely high energy level. These individuals have a hard time staying focused or maintaining limits. They may overspend, or they may have problems with sleeping. They may also have a very rapid speech pattern. Sometimes they are referred to as being "off the wall" with so much energy. Some individuals move back and forth between mania and depression.

E. Some individuals wear their feelings on their sleeve to an inappropriate degree. They are insecure and tend to need constant reassurance. There is a tendency to overemphasize and overreact to every little, real, or perceived wrong, hurt, or snub. Sometimes the word "histrionic" is used to describe people who exaggerate their feelings and appear to need a constant source of drama in their lives. There are also individuals who experience their feelings in the same exaggerated way but are quite passive. These individuals might "forget" an appointment, or spill something rather than reacting openly to their feelings.

F. "Co-dependence" is now a frequently used label in the counseling profession. Co-dependents develop in dysfunctional families, and emotionally dysfunctional families have been around for a long time. These individuals usually have a hard time setting limits, have a difficult time with boundaries, experience a lot of guilt, and often attach to incompatible mates. They may have problems with eating, alcohol, or sex. Generally, they are co-dependent on someone else as they feel they have little personal power. Co-dependents give away their power because they fear being alone or being involved in conflict. Usually they have fears of being seen in the truest sense of being seen. Of course, their fears and behaviors further their sense of insecurity and helplessness. There are now many books about co-dependence, and this highlighting has been quite useful in the understanding of dysfunctional families.

G. Dissociation is an experience of feeling unattached or not fully real. Dissociated individuals may feel as if someone else is in their body or they have no feelings. Sometimes, they describe themselves as robots. There may be periods of time when there is no sense of meaning or experience.

H. Psychosis refers to people who have lost contact with reality as most people know reality. Obviously, this is a very serious disturbance. These people may believe that they are someone other than themselves, even someone famous. They might have extreme fears of someone hurting them. Usually, these individuals hear voices or see things others do not hear or see. Professional consultation is crucial in such situations. Psychosis is quite serious and typically requires medication to control the disturbance. While some individuals never recover or only partially recover from this condition, others do return to ordinary functioning.

It is quite possible for each of us to experience some of the above. It is fairly easy to lose our sense of balance and to lose track of what our mind is telling us. It is also easy for our minds to lose track of what our feelings are telling us. The point is to recognize when this is happening and how often it is happening. This ensures we can maintain a true sense of reality in which there is a balance of emotional truths and emotional reactions.

Feelings are energies from our spirit. They can be powerful and enlivening in their constructive use. I hope these words will help you to be powerful and alive in your own experience. If your feelings are destructive, please get involved with a mental health consultant. Through therapy and possibly medications, your life can be quite different.

NOTE: While emotional well-being clearly impacts your daily living, it also affects your physical well being. Evidence is rapidly accruing that mental well-being reduces the impact of medical utilization as well as affecting recovery from surgery. For example, "Patients who participated in a biofeedback training and stress management program reported two years later a 70% reduction in visits to physicians."[5] "Patients receiving focused mental health treatment reduced overall medical costs by 22% over a year and a half, while costs rose by 22% for those not offered mental health treatment." [6] "People who experience chronic anxiety, long periods of sadness and pessimissm, unremitting tension, or incessant hostility, relentless cynicism or suspiciousness, were found to have double the risk of disease—including asthma, arthritis, headaches, peptic ulcers, and heart disease."[7] A study in the Journal of the American Medical Association found that people with narrowed heart arteries who responded abnormally to mental stress testing were nearly three times more likely than patients with normal responses to have heart attacks, require bypass surgery, or die over the next five years."[8] Emotional well-being and processing clearly affects the way you and your child live— including physical health.

Chapter 7

DISCIPLINE AS TEACHING

Questions of discipline are part of the daily parental routine. Of course, there should be questions but not in the way most parents ask. Most parents want to know "what to do" and what is "the right thing" when it comes to discipline. Questions such as these are premature without a solid relationship foundation. As a result, the topic of discipline comes late in this book. My intent was to first provide you with an understanding of the processes which contribute to healthy constructive relationships. Without your understanding the process of constructive relationships, you are less likely to be fully available to your child. Being fully available is essential to your child's knowledge that she will not be emotionally or physically abandoned. Being fully available is essential for the daily "practice" of loving your child. While love is an essential feeling, there must be a translation of this in your interactions—the love must be felt. Without the foundation of a good relationship, your discipline is likely to be ineffective and may even have long-term detrimental effects.

At the same time, there are often problems with knowing what to do about discipline, even within healthy relationships. A good relationship does not ensure problem-free parenting. You would be wise to expect difficulties and to use difficulties as opportunities for learning. Let me repeat myself, since this is a very difficult idea for most parents. You can expect to have problems and you can use these problems to teach alternative behaviors and positive values. I strongly encourage you to be a teaching parent and provide an atmosphere where your child can gradually, and at her own pace, learn to

163

be a responsible human being. You can both be tolerant of mistakes and know when mistakes become an excuse.

It is pretty incredible what the word discipline has come to mean. In fact, your first reaction may be to disagree with me. Typically, people think about reward and punishment when they think of discipline. In fact, one thesaurus suggests that to discipline one "chastises, corrects, penalizes, punishes, drills, instructs and trains." A philosophy that does not teach internal control simply reinforces rebelliousness and a sharp eye for whether the authority figure is watching. External rewards and punishments alone have not been particularly successful in teaching internal control.

One reason for the difficulty is reward-punishment strategies have an authoritarian stance with one group of people being superior to another. (Dreikurs and Grey[1] articulate a similar thought). I certainly would agree that children need to learn through their experience, but viewing them as inferior is a serious mistake. Intentionally or unintentionally we often give our children mixed messages about their value—we often communicate inferiority. Many of these messages occur in the form of negative communication. There are other mixed messages about value. For example, asking a child to hurry into adulthood while punishing her for mistakes. Please consider the possible perceptions arising from your actions. Your actions may speak louder than words in the communication of value.

A second reason for the difficulty in reward-punishment strategies is outlined by Dreikurs and Grey.[2] Children are intensely aware of issues of fairness and equality, and they strongly question the fairness of their parent's decisions. They also question the lack of fairness in the world.

My own experience would suggest a third reason why rewards and punishments are unsuccessful in teaching adequate internal control. Rewards and punishments allow children the opportunity to focus on their parents as appliers of consequences rather than upon themselves as behavers. (Dreikurs and Grey refer to this concept in a similar way). Children, then, see their parents as being responsible for the outcomes of their behavior. Your child can then focus more on what you do, rather than on her own behavior. When this happens, she then misses the point, fails to learn control, and is likely to be resentful. While you can control your child's behavior in the short run, you become her external agent of control.

A better way to teach would be to get children to connect their behavior with their internal experiences so they are more personally involved. When this happens, control truly comes from within. I believe as a culture, we know this. There is good reason for the saying "Experience is the great teacher."

Dreikurs and Grey[3] have devised such a system, and they call it "natural and logical consequences." In terms of philosophy and practice, this system attempts to connect behavior with internal experience. It also acknowledges mutual rights and respect so that the potential for resentment is minimized. Basically, this means parents serve as a guiding source to their child, rather than an all-knowing, all-seeing authority figure. As a guiding source, parents can help her to see the connections of her behavior with her experience. This provides the basis for internal learning and gives the message that her internal experience is connected to what she does, what she thinks and what she feels. It is from this vantage point that the following is written.

1. USE DISCIPLINE FOR TEACHING.

It is easy to confuse discipline as teaching with discipline as punishment. If you will think about how you would like to be taught, this confusion will disappear, and you can create respectful guidelines for teaching.

I would like to give you some of my own "don'ts." I doubt you would want teaching that made you feel bad about yourself. I doubt you would want to learn from someone who was constantly changing his mind about what he wanted. I do not think you would want someone who threatened you or called you names. I doubt you would want someone who became easily angry with your insufficient progress. I doubt you would want to learn from someone who was always reminding you of your mistakes.

These behaviors neither foster pleasant learning relationships nor encourage learning of internal control. Unpleasantness encourages the focus to be on the pain and the external reasons for the pain, not the connections between behavior and experience. Unpleasantness diminishes the desire to learn through painful associations to the learning experience.

On the other hand, discipline as teaching fosters pleasant relationships through encouraging self-esteem, consistency, and a mutual respect for caring. Discipline as teaching is understanding your child will make mistakes, and, at times, she may not try as hard as you would like. Discipline as teaching is instilling the concept that the outcome of her learning is based upon the effort she puts into the task. These qualities of teaching allow your child to be responseable and to understand what occurs when she responds one way versus another. She understands she is integral in the decision-making process and others are involved in the outcome of her decisions.

When you use discipline as teaching, you have accepted a very difficult task. It is extremely important you prepare yourself for this task and you understand your own attitudes about teaching. Children do absorb what they are exposed to. If you practice what you teach, your children will absorb a "model" relationship. Discipline as teaching is something valuable to be passed on to the next generation. A respectful, loving relationship will enhance your child's self-esteem and encourage her to want to learn as a way of growth.

2. YOUNG CHILDREN ARE ESPECIALLY SENSITIVE TO DISCIPLINE.

Young children are especially sensitive, period. This does not mean they can not learn when they are in pain, but pain may cause them to view themselves as bad or unloved. At times, your child may have very negative feelings toward you. It is your task to help your child learn what to do with her feelings. Hopefully, she will learn to accept these without guilt and to see her painful feelings as a part of the learning process.

As is appropriate, let her know that you understand her strong feelings, that it is OK to express these constructively, and that her feelings naturally accompany **her** need to behave differently. You may need for her to behave differently; but until she needs to change, you are just an authority figure. She will learn this through a sense

166

of caring about the relationship and not because of guilt. Through this constructive process, she will learn her behavior influences the world in certain ways. She will also learn she is not responsible for the way the world responds. Your love also means, when necessary, you will also see to it she does what is in her best interest.

3. THERE ARE INDICATIONS FOR A CHANGE IN DISCIPLINE (TEACHING).

As a teacher of discipline, you can look for signs of difficulty and a need to re-evaluate your approach. If, for example, there are frequent power struggles, your child is likely to be viewing you as an authority figure. If you suspect your child is out to get you, you could be right. It could be your child is getting even with what she perceives as **punishing** tactics. Another sign is when your intervention results in either no change in frequency or an increase in frequency of a certain misbehavior (over a significant period of time). Excessive fears, guilt, anger, sadness, and anxiety are signs you do not feel comfortable with your mode of discipline. If you don't feel anything about your teaching, then you are missing some very important aspects of the teaching experience. If your methods of discipline vary greatly within short periods of time, your child is not receiving consistent messages.

If you are threatening consequences you do not intend to enforce, you are not in control of your inner reactions. Of course, your inner reactions will affect your outer reactions. Chances are then good your child will subconsciously, if not consciously, feel her power in your loss of control. Your child can then learn to "push your buttons." This is one of the most important indicators that it is time to change your mode of discipline as well as to do some soul-searching. Please be alert to possible signs that your teaching as discipline is not working well or that you are not using teaching as discipline.

NOTE: If you use discipline as teaching, most of your experiences will be positive. Of course, there will be frustrations and negative impulses. There may be times when you feel completely out of control. Hopefully, you will be in enough control to minimze damage.

It is critical you keep these experiences at a minimum and outweigh the negative with positive, loving, constructive experience.

4. CONSIDER THE POSSIBLE REASONS FOR MISBEHAVIOR.

Dreikurs and Cassel [4] refer to four basic reasons for misbehavior: 1. to get attention; 2. to struggle for power; 3. to get revenge; 4. to withdraw because of feelings of inadequacy and/or discouragement. Knowing why a child is misbehaving is invaluable in deciding what to do. It helps you understand your child's process while keeping your goals in perspective. Take the time to consider her motives before you react impulsively. Do not expect her to tell you why she did something. This is often hard for adults. Instead, ask questions related to the four motives. For example, you could ask, "Did you feel I was not giving you enough time or attention?" Or you might ask, "Were you so mad that you wanted to get even?" Asking questions related to the four motives may not result in answers. Thoughtful questions and respectful interchange will provide her with a framework for thinking about her behavior which may unlock the feelings behind her behavior. Discussion and acceptance of these feelings will enhance the process of establishing internal controls.

5. AVOID PHYSICAL PUNISHMENT.

I have long believed there are two kinds of power. One is hierarchical power which comes from your position or role in life. Examples of this are being a manager, a company president, a Major in the Army and so on. These positions carry weight and responsibility just by virtue of the position. The other form of power is personal. This power comes from within and does not depend on your position of authority. While in the Army I was taught to respect the position of authority, but you may or may not respect the person. While this way of thinking may get things done in the military, it does not work well within the family. One way in which people attempt to make it work is to rely on physical punishment to create fear. **LITTLE OR NO RESPECT COMES TO A PARENT RE-**

LYING ON THE FEAR OF PHYSICAL PAIN TO MOTIVATE A CHILD.

Fear of pain requires ongoing dependency on parental authority; is disrespectful of human relationships, creates resentfulness, and possibly hatred. There is no sense of personal power or personal interaction when fear is the primary motivator. Discipline as teaching is not a case of "sparing the rod and spoiling the child." Discipline as teaching is a process of teaching people to deal with one another in respectful ways and not through who is the biggest and strongest. You do not encourage internalization of teaching if you rely on fear.

Please notice that I have used the word "avoid" in the title of this section rather than the word "never." As you know, there are no absolute rules and there may be a very rare occasion when you **deliberately** decide to use spanking. If you have established a positive relationship or are in the process, there are only two occasions I can imagine for the use of physical punishment. One is when your child is young, and this might be needed to emphasize imminent danger. The other is to assert your parental authority as a back-up to positive teaching methods.

I am not being contradictory in asserting you have parental authority that needs to be exercised in the context of mutuality. As a rare back-up you might consider spanking. But first be sure you have thought through the reasons why your child is misbehaving and your teaching methods. Please be in control of yourself if you do resort to this type of consequence. If you are going to be a successful parent, you will rely on mutual respect.

6. STAY IN CONTROL.

Your personal power is the primary teacher of behaviors, feelings, and thinking that are beneficial to your child. Being in control is essential to this effort, and being out of control undermines your attempts. Yet, as I stated earlier, you can be in control even when you are out of control. Please remember, you can monitor your being out of control so you stay within contained limits and allow your energies to flow constructively. Your child does need guidance, and

I believe she will be more content if she knows and has the guidance to operate within the rules. Guidance and control are indications you care.

This guidance and control means you know whether or not you are standing on "solid ground" and when it is conducive to collaborate. Being in control means knowing when your talking is turning into lectures or manipulations. Being in control means you are "pushing" her sense of responsibility and you are owning yours. It means you are both firm and loving. It means that you remain both emotionally objective and subjective in your discipline as teaching. Being in control means you do not let your child blackmail you. Last, but not least, being in control means responding to the serious misbehaviors and ignoring the trivial ones, unless they lead to more serious difficulties. This distinction allows you to decide when and to which behaviors you will respond. Subjectively, you will feel in more control and have a greater sense of peace.

7. USE NATURAL AND LOGICAL CONSEQUENCES.

Your parental task is to balance allowing your child to motivate herself in most instances, and setting limits if she continuously fails to do so. Of course, you will set limits in any dangerous situation. I believe an important way to achieve this balance is to use Dreikurs and Grey's method known as "natural and logical consequences." This method provides a powerful way to remove yourself as the reason for your child's having "unpleasant" experiences. In this way, your child personally experiences and learns from life opportunities.

This method acknowledges that you are your child's parent and you begin as the most important person to her. It means a very intense bond is likely to form that will be tested as she matures. This means you can collaborate with your child and lead her on her path of development. It means that while you provide limits and consequences to help her learn, your limits allow her to view these experiences as a part of herself. She is not likely to do this if your primary role is to motivate and to be her external authority.

Basically, using this method **often** means doing little or nothing and staying out of the way. You are allowing her to learn from pleasant and unpleasant experiences. As your child grows, she will learn quickly to wear warm clothes in the winter and cool clothes in the summer. Young children quickly learn how to walk from the feedback they receive from falling down. As a parent, you try to keep any sharp objects out of their path but you allow the natural development of walking. You might offer comfort for your child's tears and encouragement to try again. The process of walking, though, is your child's. You are involved, but the motivation and the learning is your child's. You are using natural consequences. Natural consequences are all those events which occur without any intervention on your part.

The trick is for your child to make the connection between her behavior and the results of her behavior. The second trick is for her to learn that her desired consequences do not always happen. We all have to learn this difficult lesson. For example, she may work for an "A" but receive a "C" in her social studies. Most of the time, though, there are direct and logical consequences to behavior. For example, if I don't work, I don't get paid. If I don't sit at this computer, nothing will go on the screen. If I don't eat, I will get hungry. If I eat, my hunger lessens.

If you will notice, nobody is doing anything to me. I am making my own choices, and the consequences are directly on my shoulders. I can not blame anybody for these consequences. To be responsible, one must be "response-able." That is, able to make responses and to understand that our responses (when we are conscious) are really choices. This is the goal of natural and logical consequences.

Some parents are uncomfortable with this method because it removes them from being the primary reason for their child's behavior. They feel they have lost control. The real question is, do you want to be the primary reason for your child's behavior? If you do, then you must accept responsibility for being her external authority figure.

I would like to give you a few practical examples of how natural and logical consequences might be used in the family. Please remember that each child and situation is different. You will have to design your own ways for utilizing natural consequences. Here are

171

some examples to consider. The first might be that when your child does not come in for dinner, she does not eat. Does this sound harsh? It depends on your full assessment. Being excessively loud would require asking her if she would like to soften or play in her room. Her excessive fighting with a brother would mean a decision to not fight or be separated. Abusing household items would mean not being allowed to use those items. Choosing to make poor grades (please see Professional Consultation chapter) would result in a withdrawal of TV until her lessons are completed. Choosing not to go to bed on time might mean preparing for bed earlier, so she can be in bed on time. Notice you are allowing your child to make choices and you are allowing her to experience the consequences of these choices.

As a parent you are interested in helping her make choices that will add to the comfort of her life and learning from the uncomfortable experiences. Dreikurs and Grey suggest you exert natural and logical consequences as a "friendly bystander,"[5] This is accomplished in a calm tone that implies regret that you "can not do anything else except to let the child face the consequences of what she has done."[6] **If you become overly invested, your child is then working for you and not for herself.** Your voice and manner must suggest that you are not getting even, but that you are quite concerned about her choices.

As you do this, you can feel your love for her learning and experiencing. With this love, she will know you are available as a guide and someone with whom to collaborate. Remember, discipline is for teaching, and this teaching is most accessible in a warm, loving atmosphere.

An angry attitude can easily lead to a power struggle and encourage her to focus on you instead of herself. An angry attitude could easily lead to your being vindictive. There will be times when there will be angry exchanges, and these can be used for experiencing and learning. You may need to rely heavily on your intellect in using and determining natural consequences to avoid punishing. I hope that you can see the benefits of teaching over punishment.

8. LOOK CAREFULLY AT PROBLEM BEHAVIORS.

As your child develops, there are likely to be certain problem behaviors that recur. Of course, this will frustrate you, and you may feel out of control. I would like to provide you with a way to regain some degree of control. First, ask yourself about the exact form of the behavior and identify it to yourself. Second, notice and evaluate the external consequences to your child when she engages in this behavior. Third, speculate about what the internal consequences might be to your child. Fourth, notice your child's responses to these consequences. This information, combined with a look at the reasons for the behavior, can be quite helpful in guiding your decisions. While you are not in complete control of your child's recurring problem behaviors, you can feel that you are approaching them in a sane way. However, by virtue of being human, you are likely to have blind spots. Try to get as much information as you can, and seek the opinions of others. You may integrate their ideas with your own to develop a way of looking at the problem behavior. You may find that this discovery process is quite rewarding.

9. THERE ARE DIFFERENT KINDS OF MISBEHAVIORS.

While this is an obvious statement, you tend to forget when your child has been difficult or when you are in a bad mood. There are also parents who feel all misbehavior is the same and will not tolerate **any** misbehavior. If you find yourself giving out the same punishments, you probably are not looking at the differences in various misbehaviors. This gives your child the impression you are not very conscious of her as a person, and you are not very serious about your parenting. It is extremely important that your decisions be conscious and good-willed. This means recognizing differences between trivial and serious misbehaviors. You would be wise to reserve your more powerful interventions for the serious misbehaviors. By reviewing (re-viewing) the process of your decisions about misbehavior, you can prevent yourself from reacting impulsively. This is a great side-effect.

173

10. WHEN POSSIBLE, CONVERT CONFLICT INTO WIN-WIN SITUATIONS.

When discipline is used for changing behavior, there is going to be conflict. Both you and your child will want to win the battle. Of course, very few people want to be losers. Losers tend not to feel good about losing and then become resentful. If this resentment becomes great, there is going to be a natural defensiveness, and future battles will become even more difficult.

A better approach is to use a win-win strategy whenever possible. This simply means you struggle with your child in the context of mutual relationship and allow her input into the improvement of the battle. In other words, you make every attempt to set up a framework so she does not feel under your thumb and has some say in the outcome. At the same time, she must come to realize that having a say does not mean escape from a solution that is in the best interest of the mutual relationship. This realization provides balance between the interests of both you and your child. If you are successful, battles will turn into negotiations and collaborations for a loving relationship. Remember, people can be angry and fight in loving ways. Please be aware of the best interests of both you and your child.

11. FOCUS ON THE FREQUENCY OF BEHAVIOR.

Focusing on the frequency of behavior does three things. One is that it reduces blaming your child for her misdeeds. Secondly, it lets you know the results of your interventions. Things are getting better, worse, or staying the same. This is tricky because you might see a rise in the frequency upon the initiation of an intervention, as she may be testing the seriousness of your intervention attempts. Be clear with yourself that what you are doing makes good sense, and stick it out for awhile to see what happens. Third, focusing on frequency can help you realize your child is not perfect nor is perfection the goal of your teaching.

12. <u>SUMMARY</u> .

There are two major principles of enhanced teaching. One is to concentrate on methods of teaching which are likely to feel good to you and your child. The other is to place responsibility for her decisions on her shoulders.

As always, there are qualifiers. As the process of teaching is quite complicated, I am suggesting two complimentary strategies. On the one hand, I am suggesting you place decision-making in your child's hands and allow her to live with the experiences that result. She will learn from these. I am also suggesting there will be times when you directly intervene and provide experiences from which she will learn. It is vitally important she understand you are doing this in her best interest and not for revenge. Mutuality is the working goal.

Chapter 8

THE GROWING EDGE

This writing began with the following words: **Children**—spirited, energetic, feeling, mysterious, imaginative, excited, dreamers, loving, fulfilled and unfulfilled promises, fearful, growing, difficult—**Qualities of Life**. These words can guide you in thinking about the real purpose of your parenting, being connected, and enhancing connectedness. This connectedness is with yourself, your spouse, your child. Being connected to your child plays a major role in her learning about life. Connectedness and love encourage the use of her full potential. Connectedness and love encourage the development of Emotional Intelligence.

Love nurtures your child as a natural resource, allows her to develop, helps her learn, and encourages her aliveness. In your loving presence, she experiences, she feels, she learns, and her spirituality unfolds. As you love her fully, you will experience much of the beauty and pain that life can bring. You and she can be a natural resource of energy, love, and kindness.

With this experience of parenting, you can experience life at its fullest. She will touch your consciousness and bring to life that which is unconscious. Parenting can readily and deeply allow you to sense your unconscious life. And from your unconscious life, you may deepen your sense of connectedness, lovingness, and aliveness. As your unconscious becomes conscious and as you struggle with your own aliveness, you will expand your boundaries; "Qualities of Life." These boundaries are your growing edge.

I like the idea of respecting your child as a natural resource.

176

She is a human being—not an object to be molded in another's image. Like a human being she flowers through love, guidance, and direction. None of us were taught how to parent. There are no schools, there are few absolute rules, and you are likely to feel overly responsible. Chances are, you have struggled with any number of questions to find answers to parenting dilemmas. I have given you few, if any, answers. My purpose has been to offer you loving, connected ways of thinking, feeling, and experiencing to create your own answers. I believe if you practice the guidelines and struggle with these ideas, your awareness and connnectedness will increase. You will become more response-able, be more fully alive, and feel more of your spirituality. Naturally, as you become more spiritual, you will be more connected and loving with your child. You, then, will be treating yourself as a natural resource.

Obviously, being connected and loving changes the process of parenting. This writing with its questions and ideas was meant to add to your "growing edge." Edges are the borders of territory—the territory of all parenting interactions. You are certainly on the edge of an emerging life. Consequently, these words are full of possibilities about the expansion of your parent-child experiences.

In fact, the words specify the experience of looking at the varieties of behavior, thinking, feeling, and spirituality within your parenting territory. As you experience your parenting, you can discover where you limit and contract from your sense of connectedness, lovingness, and aliveness. As you become conscious and aware of how you limit and contract, you may then allow your connectedness to expand. This is where you will find new possibilities in experiencing and loving. The points of expansion become your new growing edge.

My goal is not to mold you, but to encourage your process of expansion. To further influence aspects of being with your child, I would like to repeat an earlier quote:

"If young people do not have a feeling of connectedness with other human beings and if they have no empathy, guilt, shame, or sense of responsibil-

ity, then ultimately the value of human life will be lost." [1]

To share this desired value, I entitled the first chapter, "Being Crazy, Loving, and the Boiled Frog Syndrome." This was my way of saying that as a culture, we devalue human life by being "crazy." I defined "crazy" as not making sense, being mean, denying reality, and portraying the world as a storybook fantasy. All of us have participated in this as a way of denying the power of our reality. This craziness filters into each of our families with our children realizing that something is wrong. If you will recall, the temperature is "heating-up," and it is all too easy not to be fully connected with ourselves or with others.

I hope that chapter resulted in your being more aware of craziness, and you will find constructive ways to make sense, be loving, and portray reality as you experience it. This decrease in craziness will not only make a difference in your life, but also in the life of our culture. The ultimate decrease in craziness will result in connectedness to the loving, open, empathetic, soulful part of ourselves. It takes great courage to experience reality as you experience it. This is a major step in expanding your growing edge. If all of us practice, we will turn the "temperature" down.

The second chapter was entitled, "What Makes People Tick." To help this complicated process make sense, I divided living into four parts: behavior, thinking, feelings, and spirituality. These four categories can become the objects of your consciousness, and allow you to more fully experience inner and outer reality. They will encourage you to live in the moment so that experiences "pass on through," you are processing your experience. Without adequate experiencing and processing, you are in the heart of "craziness."

Experiencing and processing is internal, and it affects us at both the conscious and unconscious levels. The way we experience and process our lives affects our behavior, feelings, thoughts, and spirituality. This, in turn, affects our sense of wholeness and self-esteem. Our increased sense of wholeness and self-esteem gives us the strength to be more connected. As we are more connected, we will expand the value of human life. The experience of life is so powerful! As we all deepen, we will have enhanced our culture's growing edge.

Chapter 3 presented parenting guidelines, beginning with the importance of awareness. Your awareness is essential to expanding your growing edge. By being aware of your thoughts, behaviors, and feelings you are able to become more conscious. More important, being aware allows you the capacity to find and strengthen your internal resources. There were guidelines on being open to truth, experiencing, emotions, love, mistakes, forgiveness, fighting, and using your history constructively. There was encouragement for you to affirm and set limits. I suggested that you have tough tightwire acts to perform while you balance your expectations, emotions, and "regrettable" behaviors. Using your awareness helps you evaluate your parenting, and allows your spouse or another to collaborate with you. If you are truly loving of yourself and of your child, you will be aware of your own guidelines and how they affect relationships. Last, but not least, please allow openness for the meaning of death. I hope you will remember the quote from Treya Wilber so you might view death from an open perspective. As you practice these guidelines, you cannot help but become more connected and find the best "answers" for your child and for yourself. They reveal your growing edge.

Chapter 4 presented ideas for enhancing a positive relationship. I would like to re-emphasize the importance of seeing your child as a developing natural resource, and yourself as the major source of guidance. This is especially true in the formative years. Being the major source of guidance may frighten you and with awareness, you may use this fear constructively. Again, the purpose of this writing is for you to expand, be more connected, and therefore, more response-able. In Chapter 4 you found guidance in giving love and affirmation, in being aware of your child's sensitivity, in thinking about your marriage, in giving balanced feedback and encouragement, and in being balanced about expectations related to guilt, testing limits and so forth. I encouraged you not to be the perfect parent, but to evaluate your experiences with yourself and family. Please be a model for the qualities you are encouraging and practice what you preach. NO CRAZINESS! Last, but not least, find time to be playful with your child. Play is so important. If you are truly loving of yourself and your child, you will do everything possible to enhance a positive relationship. This is the growing edge for both you and your child.

Communication was the next topic. Naturally, communication is the bridge between you and others, you and your child. If communication is going to be the bridge, you must first have good communication with yourself. This means knowing what you really think and feel. Please remember the quote, **"My living becomes split between image and reality, between what I think I am, and what I am."**[2] If you do not know and understand your inner self, you cannot communicate what is in your inner self. This is very important in being connected. As you connect with your inner self, you encourage your child to connect with her inner self. Basically, you are encouraging your child to express her deepest thoughts and feelings in a respectful way. There was a discussion of assertive, aggressive, and passive communication. I encouraged you to communicate respectfully. This does not mean an avoidance of anger.

Please avoid the "should's," "ought's," and power struggles. When you are in doubt, clarify. Remember, there is no such thing as silence, only communication without words. Be careful when criticizing and be alert to distortions in communication. LISTEN, listen with both ears and to what you might be hearing between the lines. Clarify, rephrase, and ask simple questions. Remember the Golden Rule as you communicate. To really love your child is to communicate with her at the deepest level. From that place, your child will know you love her. To communicate with your child is your growing edge.

For most people, including myself, experiencing emotions is **the growing edge**. The emotionality chapter symbolizes aliveness. Feelings are the undercurrent of our aliveness; feelings are energies pouring from the spirit. While words do not give adequate justice to the depths of these feeling energies, we do have symbols to guide and direct our awareness.

I began by describing two psychological journeys and how these journeys bring freedom, aliveness, and wholeness. You could see the relevence to self-esteem, wholeness, and finding the real self.

Without feelings, there is deadness and a tendency toward addiction. Consquently, there is a lot of psychological energy that goes unconsciously into addictions. It is no wonder addictions are so tough to break. We all have experienced the pressure to bolster the illusion of a happy, joyful life.

As you struggle with emotionality, remember feelings serve as the human thermostat, and the difference between feeling and doing. Feelings are the energies that come with and result from experience. If you have painful feelings, you have had painful experiences. Pain in the context of reality is a natural experience. There is pain and suffering in this world, and denial results in portraying the world as a storybook fantasy. While feelings may give you the sense you are out of control, you are in control by letting feelings pass through constructively.

Please remember, if you block, you cause these energies to be numbed and to go into the unconscious. While in the unconscious, you have very little, if any, control over these energies. As a result, these energies can then "hit" you with difficult behaviors, thoughts, and feelings. My sense is that bringing these energies into consciousness will allow you more freedom to acknowledge, understand, and free them in a way that will lift their burden. You are likely to find yourself feeling "lighter" once you have accomplished this goal.

I shared with you the importance of sadness, anger, anxiety, and jealousy. These feelings are very much a part of childhood as well as adult experience. Sadness is so important as it signifies and allows the grieving of loss. Anger is scary in that so much of the culture is into revenge. There are many constructive ways to release anger, and our children can learn these ways. Anxiety signifies that something is not quite right, whole, or that there is danger. If you feel anxiety, please consider the reasons, so that you can eventually resolve this state. Jealousy refers to the feeling of someone else having something you want. Of course, this is followed by resentment. Again, this feeling, along with the other three, can be used to see yourself more clearly and allow you to explore the origins of the feelings. Amazingly, much can happen as you let yourself just be. The being frees and guides you. Being allows you to find more and more of your inner self.

A few cautions are in order about emotionality. Some people use feelings as tools for manipulation or as an excuse for destructive behavior. This is not being, but destructive doing. Analyze and work with overreactions in the family. Usually, these are congruent with unfinished business. In a family partnership, feelings are to be explored and resolved in a mutually beneficial fashion. Remember that your child will have many intense emotional reactions, and your task is to give guidance in letting these pass through.

As you feel and "pass on through," you will experience aliveness. Emotional freedom is essential to your sense of wholeness and completeness. Dealing constructively with feelings is the growing edge for you and your child. Feelings are a fuel for your spirit. In loving yourself and your child, you will do everything possible to enhance the constructive experience of feelings.

The Discipline chapter was held until the end as a way of emphasizing the need for relationship, communication, and emotionality in your parenting. In discipline as teaching, relationship is more important than control. This simply means that as you teach, your guiding principle is to enhance the parenting relationship as much as possible. In other words, you are "available" and "present" so you and your child can know how you will learn together. From that place of mutual security, you then can place yourself in your child's "shoes" and decide what is best for the two of you. As you are "available" and "present," you then realize the process of teaching is more important than your desired goal. You fully realize the process will determine whether you reach the desired goal. You know your child is sensitive to the differences in roles and in physical size. You also know that she is not your "mirror image" and to overinvest in control would sabotage your teaching efforts. Over-investment could result in her being overly responsible and not response-able. Acknowledge that she will test limits, and you can often use a Win-Win strategy to enhance a sense of collaboration for mutual good. Ask yourself questions about how you would want to be taught, remembering she is not you.

Teaching is not a series of reward-punishment strategies. Discipline in its truest sense is teaching and learning with mutual respect and limits. Teaching fosters a pleasant relationship, constructive handling of feelings, and good communication. Teaching fosters the qualities of life which enable aliveness. With this in mind, you are truly expanding the growing edge of your child.

However, it goes without saying that problems will arise in your parenting. Some of them you will be able to deal with, and some of them may be beyond your abilities. When they are beyond your abilities, I hope that you will consult with a professional congruent with your concerns. Getting the right professional will expand your growing edge of possibilities.

Chapter 9

PROFESSIONAL CONSULTATION

"By accepting you as you are, I do not necessarily abandon all hope of your improving." [1]

"One can't surmount a painful experience unless one first faces it directly." [2]

About 47 percent of Americans feel they don't know enough about when it's appropriate to see a mental health professional and 68 percent don't know how they should go about seeking help if they need it." [3]

The first quotation is worth repeating. "By accepting you as you are, I do not necessarily abandon all hope of your improving." I am sure you have heard a lot about the importance of acceptance, and true acceptance is important and well meaning. In fact, the acceptance of your child's thinking and feeling is a primary determinant of your relationship. Of course, simple acceptance is not enough. Simple acceptance of your own behavior is also not enough.

Life is full of change and growth. There is an old saying that anything that stays the same is either dead or in the process of dying. Consequently, one part of your job is to accept your child as she is, and the other part is to help her develop and learn. As you "walk" this journey, you will see that both of you develop, learn, and become more alive human beings. However, as you do this, you may

184

find you have questions you can not answer. This chapter is meant to give you permission and encouragement for seeking professional help. This professional help may be either for yourself or for your child.

Typically, most people exhaust their inner resources before considering professional consultation. They attempt to struggle with resistance to change, insecurity, and look for quick solutions to behavioral problems. We, as a culture, still believe that we can do it ourselves. I'm sure you have heard the phrase, "pull yourself up by the bootstraps." Do not let what others might think or your own hesitant concerns get in your way. There are problems you cannot expect to handle alone, and professional consultation is likely to help. Last, but not least, do not allow anyone the opportunity to try to punish your child's problems out of existence. This only drives the difficulties "underground."

In Section 1, I provide you with a list of behaviors which indicate the need for professional consultation for either you or your child. While the list is primarily child oriented, any problems or processing difficulites of your own may also be examined for professional need. This is for your own sense of well being as well as minimizing the risk of your child's "absorbing" any of these difficulites. The list is not exhaustive, and I would ask you to be aware of anything that continues to bother you. If you do not seek help, please remain aware of whether or not the problem has improved after a month's time. If it has not, please reconsider your decision.

Section 2 provides a brief discussion of learning disabilities and hyperactivity. Many of these difficulties are now called "attention deficit disorders." This section was written with the help of Dr. Michael Wesson, a specialist in this area at the University of Alabama at Birmingham.

Sections 3, 4, 5, 6, 7, and 8 deal with different therapeutic approaches. This is a convenient grouping for discussing a few of the many possible therapeutic approaches. Each professional is likely to adapt an approach suitable to his or her own personality style and, ideally, to the needs of the particular person or family seeking help. Some are more suited to children, and some are more suited to adults. You will want to have some basic understanding of the approach that most likely will fit your needs.

1. BEHAVIORS AND/OR INCIDENTS SUGGESTING THE NEED FOR PROFESSIONAL CONSULTATION FOR YOU OR YOUR CHILD

Excessive fears of school or of trying new things.
Frequent nightmares not eased by reassurance.
Sudden and/or prolonged sadness and anger.
Sudden and/or prolonged withdrawal (possible depression).
Excessive complaints of stomach problems or headaches.
A sudden or gradual change in grades.
Poor concentration or short attention span.
Problems with reading.
Being consistently difficult to get along with.
Other relationship problems.
Excessive signs of anger and defiance.
Excessive desires to be perfect.
Excessive signs of anxiety, insecurity, or inadequacy.
Excessive signs of guilt.
Prolonged recovery from a death of a friend, family member, or pet.
Eating disorders of any nature.
Occurrence of incest or rape.
Occurrence of physical or emotional abuse.
Excessive fearfulness of separation.
Experience of any traumatic event.
Difficulties with toileting behavior that are age inappropriate.
Delayed age-appropriate behaviors such as speech.
Stealing or other socially inappropriate behavior.
Problems with being excessively under or overweight.
Loss of contact with reality.
Any use of foreign or illegal substances.

If your child has or has had any of these behaviors or experiences, she is also likely to have self-esteem problems. She is likely to have anxiety, feelings of alienation, and difficulties with self-confidence. This is often translated into the childhood feeling of "badness." It is not unusual for children to see themselves as bad when bad things are happening to them. This would be her "magical" way of trying to get some sense of control. Please do not reinforce the confusion between bad things and her being "bad." You and your child can collaborate on how best to deal with the situation. Collaboration is the most likely way for the two of you to resolve the situation. You may provide gentle and strong guidance within this collaboration.

2. LEARNING DISABILITES AND ATTENTION DEFICIT DISORDERS

Many children who do not perform as expected (in school) are crying for help or have difficulties out of their control. Mind you, this is seldom conscious behavior, and it will probably do no good to blame or get angry. Parents are likely to become concerned when their child is not performing at the expected grade level, and this is understandable. Without intervention, children will get further and further behind while their self-esteem suffers. I refer to this as recycling failure, and this failure may have multiple causes. Generally speaking, poor school performance is usually the result of problems with intellectual capability, emotional problems, learning disabilities, and attention deficit disorders. It could be primarily one of these or a particular combination. Intellectual capability can be measured by a psychologist. Emotionality has been the general topic of this writing, so I need not say more. This leaves the areas of learning disabilities and attention deficit disorders.

If you have a child who is having trouble in school, professional consultation is well advised. However, I suggest that you proceed in a very cautious manner in seeking a solution. This caution comes from the general, cultural orientation of trying to find the quickest and easiest solution. As you well know, this is not always best. I would suggest a thorough intelligence examination as well as a visual-motor screening such as the Bender Visual Motor Gestalt Test. In terms of physical possibilities, a thorough evaluation by your child's pediatrician is essential along with a hearing and eye evaluation.

Typically, the term "learning disability" refers to a child who intellectually is average or better, but who has a deficit in one or more of the traditional learning areas (reading, mathematics, writing skills). This raises the question as to why a child would be of average intelligence and yet not function as such in some areas. Some professionals refer to the deficit as a delay, since this learning has not "kept up" with other areas. There can be many reasons for the delay, and one reason may stem from difficulties with the sensory system of vision. Vision difficulties can be divided into four areas: 1. the physical health of the eye; 2. the need for glasses (refractive error); 3. how well the two eyes work together (binocular coordination); 4. how well a child can actually use the information taken in through the eyes (visual-perceptual skills). Most eye practitioners consider the first two areas to be their primary concern. However, eye coordination and visual-perceptual skill deficits can also create serious difficulties.

The coordination of the eyes and the ability to use visual information are crucial to your child's classroom performance. If your child is reporting blurred vision, headaches, or if there is evidence of letter reversals after the ages of seven or eight, please consult a specialist with expertise in visual-perceptual difficulties. If your child is having difficulties with reading, compared to her intellectual capability, have her evaluated.

The ability to process visual information and then reproduce this information through writing is known as visual-motor coordination. This term can be used for other concerns, but it is most important for classroom activities. There is no doubt that a child with problems in any of these areas cannot perform at her best level. Typically, children are not aware of these problems, but do have a vague sense of something being wrong. For example, one child unintentionally distorted her dysfunctional eye in a human-figure drawing. This vague knowing and the lack of ideal school performance can then lead to emotional difficulties, and, of course, lessen a child's self-esteem. From this brief discussion, you can see that visual problems can lead to serious difficulties.

Please think about what you would be like if you were experiencing these types of difficulties. Chances are that you would lose confidence, not want to try, become fidgety, and have difficulty concentrating. These are major ingredients of hyperactivity or attention deficit disorder. There is also a second consideration in hyperactivity—the consideration of temperment. There is no doubt that some children have higher levels of energy than others and some children have trouble keeping this energy under control. These are also components of hyperactivity and attention deficit disorders.

Basically, hyperactivity and attention deficit disorder are words which label and describe. The term "attention deficit disorder" refers to a child who: 1. can not sustain age-appropriate attention for any length of time; or 2. who seems to be "on the move" more frequently than her peers. In the extreme version, adults refer to this as "climbing the walls." These words do NOT explain why. There are many possible causes, including biochemical imbalances, genetic difficulties, pregnancy difficulties, intellectual capability, emotionality, developmental delays, food allergies, television, lead, balance and coordination problems, and so on. Without a thorough evaluation, it is very difficult to know the roots of classroom difficulties.

There are many professionals who believe these difficulties stem from problems for which medications **must** be used. Medications for behavioral control can be useful (and sometimes essential), but only subsequent to a thorough evaluation of your child. While medications can be effective and immediate in their effects, they may cover up other difficulties your child is experiencing. As *Newsweek*[4] has suggested, "diagnosing attention deficit remains as much art as science." I strongly advocate psychological therapy for a child on behavioral control medications. Again, *Newsweek*[5] notes, "But most of the surveyed pediatricians said they rarely recommend anything more than pills." Please take classroom difficulties very seriously and pursue a comprehensive evaluation of your child. This comprehensive examination will be very helpful to your decision making.

THERAPY APPROACHES

3. BEHAVIORAL APPROACH

This approach has its roots in the psychology lab and is strongly oriented toward a scientific point of view. Its major focus is on behaviors which can be seen and measured. However, this approach has been extended to the reporting of internal events, such as particular thoughts. Generally, a behaviorist is concerned with a specific problem behavior and the situational factors which both precede and follow it. There is not likely to be much emphasis on the underlying feelings and motivations. Generally behaviorists believe, that as behavior changes, the feelings will also change. Usually, there is a great deal of emphasis on recording the behavior's frequency to notice how the frequency changes. Behaviorists have an interest in increasing wanted behaviors and decreasing unwanted behaviors.

Behaviorists do a great deal of work in the area of phobias and stress. Their emphasis is on replacing the fear and stress with a very pleasant image or a feeling of relaxation. This is accomplished by asking a client to visualize pleasant things or to relax the body muscles. Behaviorists also use systematic desensitization, which involves giving a client a graded series of fear-provoking images. These are given in an order which starts with little fear and progresses to images provoking higher levels of fear. The client mentally visualizes the image and then uses relaxation to lessen the fear.

Behaviorists are now using scientific principles to deal with other problem matters. One extension of the behavioral approach is something called "covert conditioning." This involves teaching a client to apply imagined consequences to internal events. For example, if you wanted to lose weight, you could imagine a trip to the beach as a reward for refusing dessert. You might also imagine yourself in an attractive swimsuit. Behavioristic approaches are most accessible to specific problem behaviors.

4. COGNITIVE APPROACH

The cognitive approach is an extension of the behavioral approach. Here the primary focus is on how thinking affects feelings and behavior. The goal is the same as in the behavioral approach— to change behavior. Cognitive therapists are interested in the types of thinking which bring a person to unwanted behavior. These therapists try to confront self-destructive or distorted thoughts and have clients see how such thinking gets in their way. They will also have clients talk to themselves about their thoughts so that their awareness level is increased. This awareness is related to when and how thoughts affect feelings and behavior. The cognitive and the behavioral approach are generally thought of as short-term therapies.

5. MEDICAL APPROACH

This approach assumes that there is something wrong with the body which can be corrected through medication. This could be neurological, hormonal, nutritional, or referred to as a biochemical imbalance. Physical problems can strongly influence one's emotional health. In using a strict medical approach, the emphasis is on the effect of medications, and there is an assumption that any accompanying social problems will change. There are "medical" professionals who will emphasize both medications and social problems. Only physicians may prescribe medicine and, as a result, the field of psychiatry is most relevant to this approach. Psychiatrists generally deal with tranquilizers, mood elevators, or other drugs with a designated purpose. Generally, psychiatrists will have other staff professionals (eg. social workers, psychologists) to deal with related psychological issues. The types and estimated time taking medications are factors in this treatment method. The potential for drug-induced side effects is another consideration.

6. FAMILY APPROACH

By virtue of its name, this approach uses as much of the family as possible to change behavior. Instead of declaring the child the

191

patient, the family process becomes the examined theme. Generally, a family therapist will focus on interactions which produce unwanted feelings and behaviors. These therapists can be very active and directive, or they can be very passive. If active, they will often ask that certain behaviors be practiced, and in some cases, they will request an increase in the unwanted behavior. This pushes clients to see the behavior differently. These therapists (and others) often have a plan or strategy which they may or may not reveal.

Family therapists are also interested in how the family cooperates, stifles, or encourages communication, works out problems, and relates emotionally. As individual members of the family change, or as the family interactions change, the unwanted behavior is likely to diminish. But as with other approaches, there may be a short-term increase in the behavior. Family therapy can be quite useful by involving the whole family in the problem. Within the family approach, there may or may not be an interest in the internal events of each member. Having a number of people in the room may increase the concentration on the external interactions. In thinking about a family therapist, you may want to inquire about the focus on external and internal events.

7. PLAY AND ART APPROACH

This is a one-on-one approach. It allows a great deal of focus on internal events. While the play and art approach can be useful with adults, it is primarily used with children. Playing and drawing help bring out thoughts and feelings in children beyond their conscious awareness. In other words, these directed activities help them unlock feelings, thinking, and behaviors that are crucial to their process. Playing and drawing allows a child to re-create a problem, bad feelings, good feelings, problem behaviors, or a problem situation without having to expose themselves to the actual problem. In other words, they can deal more safely with reality through the use of play and symbols. With adults, the equivalent would be achieved in fantasy (although art can be used). Through the use of play and symbols, children can gain mastery over problem situations, release emotional feelings, and increase their eye-hand coordination. At the same time, a child can develop a relationship with another person outside the family. This can give her a sense of safety, as well as an opportunity to examine her own internal process. This sense of safety is very important to children and adults.

8. <u>DYNAMIC APPROACHES</u>

This covers a wide variety of approaches. They are called "dynamic" in that they deal extensively with how your psychological parts both work together and create tension with one another. Specific problems arise through the conflict of psychological parts. Analysis occurs both at the mental and the emotional level. Some therapists also encourage looking at spiritual dynamics.

Each dynamic approach has its own particular emphasis and methods; however, there are several common factors. One is a heavy emphasis on childhood emotional experiences. It is assumed that early patterning of emotions continues into adulthood. This is not for blaming or for making excuses, but for achieving greater understanding. With analysis, these patterns can become more ingrained or changed, depending on the desired results.

The power of the unconscious to influence behavior is a second common factor. Generally, therapists will utilize dream interpretation and free association to give greater access to the unconscious. Dream interpretation is looking at the meaning of your dreams, deciding upon their significance and obtaining their message. Free association is letting your mind have "free rein" and saying whatever comes into your mind. Within the dynamic approach there is an emphasis on the relationship between the professional and the client (in some circles they are called patients). The assumption is that people will reenact all parts of themselves in all kinds of situations, including therapy. Of course, the professional also brings his or her own personality into the relationship. You may want to know if the professional has been in therapy. Many dynamic approaches encourage therapists to be in therapy in order to aid their own growth and sensitivity. From the professional /client relationship, both individuals can discover more of their internal selves, and the relationship can serve as a resource of healing psychological wounds. From

193

this discovery and healing, there can be a change in attitude, behavior, thinking, feeling, and spirituality.

Dynamic approaches are broad-based personality approaches and do not emphasize specific problem behaviors. However many specific problems correct through the use of this model. Dynamic therapies typically involve self-realization, self-fulfillment, and balance between thinking and emotions. As you would guess, these approaches involve a longer period of time than "brief" therapies. While the personality of the professional is important in all approaches, it is critical in the dynamic approach.

9. CHOOSING A PROFESSIONAL

There is a great deal of information to consider when you begin to seek professional consultation. First, I would ask you to review your observations of the problem and consider how the problem came to be. You might write a history of the difficulty. This information will play a role in choosing the type of approach. You may have vague thoughts about the nature of the difficulty or you may have very concrete and extensive ideas. This thinking will be important to give to the professional as a part of history-taking. If you do not have any ideas, the professional will help you develop some through his or her questions.

The second step is for you to consider whether you simply want to eliminate the problem or to explore personality issues that might have created the problem. This is an extremely important question. This question also concerns whether you want short-term (3-20 visits) or longer-term therapy (6 months to two years). Another related question is whether you want a professional who is technical in orientation or one who is more free-flowing. The way you think and feel about life will play a role in your treatment choices. Your treatment choice could affect the way you think and feel about life.

As you answer these and any other questions you might have, you will determine the approach most comfortable for you. From here you can obtain referrals from other informed individuals who can tell you about particular professionals and their approaches. If you cannot find informed sources, then you might use phone consultations with various professionals to obtain this information. Most professionals will be glad to provide a short telephone consultation. Your Mental Health Association is another source of information.

I hope this brief discussion enables you to sense which approach might be most effective for your situation. The decision is extremely important and will have a profound effect on both you and your child. Getting "help" is essential with difficulties beyond your control or with problems that you have been unable to change.

Acceptance and awareness is a place of beginning, a place of growth. Awareness and growth enhance the experience of connected life. Connectedness encourages you to live your life more fully. Professional consultation can help you remove the blinders and obstacles to growth. The following example documents the effects of disconnected parenting into adult life and then, onto the next generation. At the same time, these effects are being curtailed and reduced through MLT's psychotherapeautic journey.

Lack of Connectedness:

MLT'S PERSONAL EXPERIENCE

MLT was a 38-year-old, divorced, successful, professional male who called for an appointment a year after his divorce. He was a very attractive man who appeared about ten years younger than his age. He came to therapy because he was not content with himself, and he was not at ease without something to occupy his mind. He further noted that "stuff" from his past interfered with his living in the present. "Stuff" included feelings about his ex-wife and his ability to deal with his children. He reported frequent annoyance, impatience, and occasional outbursts of anger with his two children. **These negative feelings and behaviors interfered with his parenting experience.** This bothered him greatly. Because he was also perfectionistic, part of him wanted to deny his disturbing feelings and behaviors. He noted he often felt inadequate, insecure, and embarrassed. He did not talk about these experiences with friends, who would be astonished to know of his feelings. He was often guilty of "black and white" thinking and wanted to be more flexible in his perceptions of the world. Last, but not least, he reported he was better at communicating in writing than face-to-face. He experienced a lack of connectedness and an ongoing sense of unfullfillment. He wanted relief and improvement in his emotional functioning.

As a child, MLT had been an "A"-"B" student in a private school within an upper middle class neighborhood. He was an excellent athlete who participated in many sports activities. His father attended most of these events, and supported him well in all achieve-

196

ment activities. However, his support always included criticism, and none of MLT's achievements measured up for experienced approval. He felt he was never "good enough."

His parents were quite forceful and controlling in their efforts to produce a model child. He was never allowed to express himself and was frequently accused of "backtalking." Once, he was switched for something he had not done. He learned quickly what to say and what not to say. Even as an adult, MLT is afraid of saying the wrong things and being "shot down." His parents still change the subject or walk out of the room if he attempts to discuss an uncomfortable subject. On the other hand, he can count on their help in ways convenient to their lifestyle.

Therapy began with an examination of his perfectionistic attitudes. He initially wanted a "quick fix" and had difficulty in identifying his feelings. He performed well at the intellectual level but stumbled as he approached his emotional side. When he thought or felt differently from what he expected, he intensely berated himself. His perfectionism went so deep that he felt guilty over one of his dreams. More specifically, he killed someone in the dream and did not realize the symbolism of inner conflict. This work led to an exploration of his humanness and gave him permission to examine the dream's essence (message). He quickly realized that certain psychological aspects were either not functioning or interfering with his freedom to function. Hence, his inability to communicate with himself and others.

As MLT re-collected early memories, he came to realize the effects of lack of encouragement, of constant reminders of his inadequacy, and his locked away feelings. Of course, this revealed the basis for his feelings of inadequacy, insecurity, and perfectionism. He began separating parental limits from his own. He became aware of parental messages and began re-creating his own. He had an ever growing realization of internal splits that kept him divided on what he felt and thought.

He now knows and feels when one part of him is obstructing the energy flow of another part. He knows when he does not feel whole and his self-esteem is lagging behind his accomplishments. **He is becoming more aware of lost opportunities for himself as**

well as for his children. He has moved away from his "quick-fix" stance and is exploring the sources of uncomfortable feelings and thoughts. He summarizes his old feelings as living without anchors; anchors of a firm relationship with himself and others.

His work has brought the awareness of the differences between conditional and unconditional love. As a result, he is more forgiving of his "mistakes." Self-forgiveness allows him to be more conscious of his underlying conflicts and feelings. By allowing these feelings to become more conscious, he feels a new freedom. These new thoughts, feelings and behaviors give him a richer, fuller sense of wholeness and self-esteem. His angry outbursts are becoming more apparent to him and are decreasing. As he becomes free of the internal splits, the relationships with his children are improving dramatically; his general experience is much more positive. He and his children are free to explore, play, walk together, and even do homework in a pleasant manner. **He feels connected and relates to his children in ways he never thought possible.** His improved communication with himself enables him to communicate with others. Most importantly, his sense of unconditional love is increasing at a rapid rate, and he has found his anchor within himself. This anchor is the foundation for his healing. He is now living life more fully. Both he and his children have benefited from his journey. His children's children will also benefit.

Our children are our most valuable resource and treasure. They ennable us to envision the qualities of life.

ENDNOTES

Preface Page

1. From *EMOTIONAL INTELLIGENCE,* by Daniel Goleman. ©1995 by Daniel
Goleman. Used by permission of Bantam Books, a division of Bantam
Doubleday Dell Publishing group, Inc. Quote from page 34.

Introduction

1. Goleman, Ibid., page 89.
2. I am and will be using the feminine pronoun to honor the feminine aspects of
relationship.
3. Goleman, Ibid., page 143.

Poet's Prayer

1. Autry, James, *Life After Mississippi,* Oxford, MS: Yoknapatawpha Press,
1989. Reprinted with permission of author.

Chapter One

1. © 1978 by Scott M. Peck, M.D. *The Road Less Traveled,* New York: Simon &
Schuster, Inc. Reprinted by permission of Simon & Schuster, Inc.
2. Touefexis, Anastasia, "Teenagers and Sex Crimes," *Time,* June 5, 1989.
3. Connectedness note.
　　　　You may be wondering about my definition of connectedness, and I
have purposely avoided this in the text. I invite you to define this word for
yourself. By thinking for yourself, you are likely to discover some important
things about your own sense of connectedness. I consider these important
discoveries about the way you live and think about life.
　　　　In terms of my definition, I define connectedness as having the ability
to experience the feelings of others in a way that allows you to have a strong
idea of what another person is feeling. With this ability, you may feel the
feeling yourself or it may remind you of a time when you felt the emotion.
Of course, you might feel very connected, just a little connected, or not
connected at all. If you do feel connected, you are likely to have a sense of
sharing with the other person or feel that there is a bridge between the two of
you. You certainly will be able to relate to the other person and feel linked to
some quality or qualities. At the very least, connectedness is the ability to
relate to others as fellow human beings in the struggle to improve our lives.
　　　　An example of connectedness was the outpouring of support to
American flood victims. Obviously, their loss touched a sense of loss in
many other individuals. It reminds me of an old saying, "There, but for the
grace of God, go I." You are likely to have other examples of connectedness.

199

4. *USA Today*, November 2, 1994.
5. "Teenage Time Bombs," *US News & World Report*, March 25, 1996.
6. Salholz, E. et. al., "Women Under Assault," *Newsweek*, July 16, 1990.
7. Gibbs, Nancy, "When Is It Rape?" *Time*, June 3, 1991.
8. *Harpers*, July 1988.
9. Ford, M.D. Charles, *Lies, Lies, Lies: The Psychology of Deceit*, Washington, D.C.: American Psychiatric Press, 1996.
10. Revel, Jean-Francois, *The Flight From Truth: The Reign of Deceit in the Age of Information*, New York: Random House, 1991.
11. Barnes, J.A., *A Pack of Lies*, Cambridge, Great Britain: Cambridge Press, 1994.
12. Saxe, Leonard, "Thoughts of an Applied Social Psychologist," *American Psychologist*, 46: 409-415, 1991.
13. *Time*, October 5, 1992, page 21.
14. *USA Today*, "Cheating, Lying on the Rise," February 23, 1996.
15. *US News & World Report*, "Drug Usage on Rise," March 25, 1996, pg 30.
16. *USA Today*, January 14, 1994.
17. *Birmingham News*, Costs of Depression," April 2, 1996.

Chapter Two

1. James, J. and James, M., *Passion for Life: Psychology and the Human Spirit*, New York: Penguin USA, 1991, page 47. Reprinted with permission.
2. Howatch, Susan, *Ultimate Prizes*, New York: Random House, 1989, page 324. Reprinted with permission.

Chapter Three

1. Blodgett, Alden, "Off to See the Wizard," *Newsweek*, April 1, 1996.
2. Moss, Richard, "The Miracle of Spiritual Evolution," *Personal Transformation*, Spring, 1996, page 78.
3. Howatch, Ibid., page 273.
4. Howatch, Ibid., page 96.
5. Laurel, personal communication.
6. Raven, Charles, *The Cross and the Crisis*, as quoted in Howatch, Ibid., page 249.
7. Reprinted from *Parabola*, The Magazine of Myth and Tradition, Vol. XI, No. 4 (Winter, 1986). Used with permission.
8. Treya Wilbur, "Love Story," *New Age*, July/August, 1989, page 32.

Chapter Four

1. Howard, Stephen, M.D., "Cartooning: How Couples Draw Life in Two Dimensions," *Pilgrimage*, 135 Sequoyah Road, Highlands NC 28741, January/February 1989, Vol 15, page 166. Reprinted with permission.

Chapter Five

1. Thoele, Sue Patton, "Sacred Communication," *Personal Transformation*, Spring 1969, page 40. Used by permission of author.
2. Stevens, John, *Awareness, Exploring, Experimenting, Experiencing*, Utah: Real People Press, 1971, page 201.
3. Thoele, Ibid.
4. Dyer, Wayne, *What Do You Really Want For Your Children*, New York: William Morrow and Company, Inc., 1985, page 197.Used with permission.
5. Thoele, Ibid., page 41.
6. Satir, Virginia, *Peoplemaking*, Palo Alto,CA: Science and Behavior Books, Inc., 1972, page 63.
7. Thoele, Ibid., page 42.
8. Heldman, Mary Lynne, *When Words Hurt*, New York: New Chapter Press, 1988, page 194. Reprinted with permission.
9. Thoele, Ibid., page 41.

Chapter Six

1. Howatch, Ibid., page 430.
2. Cori, personal communication.
3.. *APA Monitor*, Volume 25, November, 1994, page 24.
4.. Moss, Ibid., page 78.
5.. Sobel, David, M.D., and Ornstein, Robert, Ph.D., *Mental Medicine Update*, Volume IV, Number 4, 1994, page 7.
6. Ibid.
7. Goleman, Ibid., page 169.
8. *U.S.A. Today*, June 5, 1996.

Chapter Seven

1. Dreikurs, Rudolph, M.D. and Grey, Loren, Ph.D., *A New Approach to Discipline: Logical Consequences*, New York: Hawthorne Books, 1968, page 254.
2. Dreikurs, Rudolph, M.D. and Grey, Loren, Ph.D., *A Parent's Guide to Child Discipline*, New York: Hawthorne Books, 1970, page 254.
3. Dreikurs and Grey, Ibid.
4. Dreikurs, Rudolph, M.D. and Cassell, Pearl, *Discipline Without Tears*, New York: Hawthorne Books/Dutton, 1972, page 34.
5. Dreikurs and Grey, Ibid., page 77.
6. Ibid., page 77.

Chapter Eight

1. Touefexis, Ibid., page 276.
2. Stevens, Ibid., page 201.

Chapter Nine

1. © Asleigh Brilliant, *Pot-Shots*, Santa Barbara, CA, 1980. Used with permission.
2. Howatch, Ibid., page 204.
3. Cantor, Dorothy, President of American Psychological Association, as quoted in *Birmingham News*, March 18, 1996.
4. *Newsweek*, March 18, 1996, page 52.
5. Ibid.

BIBLIOGRAPHY

Autry, James, *Life After Mississippi,* Oxford, MS: Yoknapatawpha Press, 1989.

Barnes, J.A., *A Pack of Lies*, Cambridge, Great Britain: Cambridge Press, 1994.

Dreikurs Rudolph, M.D. and Cassell, Pearl, *Discipline Without Tears*, New York: Hawthorne Books/Dutton, 1972.

Dreikurs, Rudolph, M.D. and Grey, Loren, Ph.D., *A New Approach to Discipline: Logical Consequences*, New York: Hawthorne Books, 1968.

Dreikurs, Rudolph, M.D. and Grey, Loren, Ph.D., *A Parent's Guide to Child Discipline*, New York: Hawthorne Books, 1970.

Dyer, Wayne, *What Do You Really Want For Your Children*, New York: William Morrow and Company, Inc., 1985.

Ford, M.D. Charles, *Lies, Lies, Lies: The Psychology of Deceit,* Washington, D.C.: American Psychiatric Press, 1996.

Goleman, Daniel, *Emotional Intelligence*, New York: Bantam Publishing Group, 1995.

Heldman, Mary Lynne, *When Words Hurt*, New York: New Chapter Press, 1988.

Howatch, Susan, *Ultimate Prizes*, New York: Random House, 1989.

James, J. and James, M., *Passion for Life: Psychology and the Human Spirit,* New York: Penguin USA, 1991.

Peck, Scott, New York: Simon & Schuster, Inc., 1978.

Revel, Jean-Francois, *The Flight From Truth: The Reign of Deceit in the Age of Information*, New York: Random House, 1991.

Satir, Virginia, *Peoplemaking*, Palo Alto,CA: Science and Behavior Books, Inc., 1972.

Stevens, John, *Awareness, Exploring, Experimenting, Experiencing*, Utah: Real People Press, 1971.

About the Author

Dr. David E. Myers is a licensed clinical psychologist in Birmingham, Alabama and has been in the practice of experiental psychotherapy for over 20 years. His background is filled with experiental work related to individuals, couples, families, gestalt therapy, bioenergetics, psychomotor, Dream body, and spirituality.

His belief system is that each of us adapt in the best way we know how, and that we carry the impressions of all of our experiences. These impressions are either conscious or affect us at levels below awareness. He works heavily with dreams and other awareness mechanisms to allow greater freedom to fulfill human potential. The remainder of his work centers on lowering or removing obstacles to fulfilling this potential.

HEARTFUL PARENTING

Dr. Christman's LEARN TO READ BOOK by Dr. Ernest Christman

A complete learn-to-read program for all ages. This highly illustrated book is a fun, yet effective way to teach anyone to read. Step-by-step the book uses the best building blocks for learning how to read.

ISBN 0-933025-17-3   256 pages $15.9

ORDER FORM

To order more books from Blue Bird Publishing, use this handy order form. For a free catalog, write to address below or check Web site: http://www.bluebird1.com

_____*Homeless! Without Addresses in America*	$11.95
_____*Home Schools: An Alternative* (4th edition)	$12.95
_____*Home Education Resource Guide* (4th ed.)	$12.95
_____*Heartful Parenting*	$14.95
_____*Home Business Resource Guide*	$11.95
_____*Dr. Christman's Learn-to-Read Book*	$15.95
_____*Look Inside: Affirmations for Kids*	$18.95
_____*Preschool Learning Activities*	$19.95
_____*Parents' Guide to Helping Kids Become*	
"A" *Students*	$11.95
_____*Divorced Dad's Handbook*	$12.95
_____*Expanding Your Child's Horizons*	$12.95
_____*Road School*	$14.95
_____*Parent's Guide to a Problem Child*	$11.95
_____*Multicultural Education Resource Guide*	$12.95
_____*Dragon-Slaying for Couples*	$14.95

Shipping Charges: $2.50 for first book. Add 50¢ for each additional book. **Total charges for books:**_____ **Total shipping charges:**_____ **TOTAL ENCLOSED:**_____	Checks, money orders, and credit cards accepted. NAME:_____ ADDRESS:_____ CITY, STATE, ZIP:_____

FOR MAIL ORDERS, complete the following:

Please charge my _____VISA _____MasterCard
Card# _____
Expiration Date: _____
Signature: _____
Phone#: _____

BLUE BIRD PUBLISHING
2266 S. Dobson #275
Mesa AZ 85202
(602) 831-6063
FAX (602) 831-1829
E-mail: bluebird@bluebird1.com
Web site: http://www.bluebird1.com